ROSE GROWING
FOR PLEASURE

ROSE GROWING

FOR PLEASURE

DEANE ROSS

LOTHIAN PUBLISHING COMPANY
MELBOURNE — SYDNEY — AUCKLAND

First published 1985
by Lothian Publishing Company Pty. Ltd.
Reprint 1986

National Library of Australia
Cataloguing-in-Publication Data:

Ross, Deane, 1930-
    Rose-growing for pleasure.

    Includes index.
    ISBN 0 85091 181 8.

    1. Roses. I. Title

635.9'33372

All black and white illustrations were drawn by
Maureen Ross and all colour photos were taken by
the author.

Designed By Derrick Stone
Typesetting By Bookset Pty. Ltd., North Melbourne
Printed By Globe Press Brunswick Vic.

Contents

Introduction

So you are interested in roses. You are in good company because roses are undoubtedly the best-known and most widely grown flower in the flower world. There must be millions and millions of rose growers caring for perhaps billions of rose plants, for roses are grown from the snowfields to the tropics and in practically all countries round the globe. Whether in magnificent parks or humble window-boxes, in trial gardens as unnamed seedlings or in ancient collections, all roses attract their devotees — indeed the devotion with which rose growers discuss their particular favourites verges on idolatry.

The genus *Rosa* is like a glittering gemstone where each facet reflects its own sparkle, each type of rose reflecting the interest of its admirer. The rose is many things to many people.

To the botanist, it is the simple, sometimes despised, wayside species, the ancestors of modern roses and cousins to apples, blackberries, hawthorn and spireas.

To the historian, the rose is the Moss rose, the Damask and Gallica rose and the Cabbage rose.

The fossicker finds roses amongst ruins and gravestones, marvelling at their hardiness and rugged beauty and searching for a clue to their identity.

To the landscaper, roses are sweeping vistas of colour, and of graceful curves and marshalled beds of elegant specimen plants.

To the competitor, the rose is the carefully nurtured and groomed bloom on the show bench, with its circular outline, spiralling petals and pointed centre.

The floral artist's rose is tastefully arranged with companion plants so that each complements the other.

The hobbyist finds the rose in pot-pourri, conserves or rose wine, as dried or preserved specimens or amongst the herbs.

The photographer sees the rose as the specimen bloom standing sharply in focus in the viewfinder.

Sweethearts sigh over the florist's bud arranged with ribbon and tinsel.

And the homemakers, that is most of us, our roses are the plants scattered throughout the garden. Some are planned, some we cannot resist and just must make room for one more, some have been gifts or grown from slips by well-meaning friends, but all in all, they make the garden colourful, fragrant and welcome.

Perhaps you are not sure which is "your" rose. If so, I hope that by reading this book you will find out. You must realize, if you do not already, that roses and rose-fanciers cannot be fitted into a mould. Naturally you have, or will find, that you develop favourites and you will feel like singing their praises to all the world, but please, please, remember that others get just as much enjoyment from their favourites, and they, too, are entitled to their tastes, unusual as they may seem to you. The rose is "big" enough to accommodate us all.

The theme of this book is the easy care and pleasure of roses. Pleasure takes many forms. There is the expectation of planning, the thrill of seeing your first buds opening, and the satisfaction of sitting back and admiring your fully mature garden. There is the browsing through the garden, snipping here, weeding a little there, seeing if any pests or diseases are raising their heads; and the big winter pruning and clean-up when you prepare for the new season. There is the joy of cutting armfuls of blooms for an important occasion, and the irresistible urge to snip a perfect bloom to share with someone.

But what of the thorns, the backaches, the spraying and the pruning? Do you call that pleasure?

It would be unrealistic of me to say that these obstacles are only in the mind, especially when you have just backed into a large thorny branch, but your attitude makes a lot of difference.

Pruning-time is when you prepare your bushes for the next season, all tidied and shaped ready to give their best. Spraying can be easier if you understand the interplay between pests and predators and their lifecycles, and other forces of nature.

Thorns are there to slow you down so that you can take time to admire the roses around you. And are the backaches any worse than the bowler's or golfer's or fisherman's ailments?

This book is the result of what other people have taught me — not one or two people, but tens of thousands of them. I grow rose plants and sell them to the public, from rank amateurs to connoisseurs. I have had the privilege over the past twenty-odd years of sharing their hopes and ideas, and their successes and problems. I have been able to follow their gardens from the first sketches on scribbling paper to maturity. These people have taught me most of what I want to pass on to you about roses. The gist of thousands of conversations has told me what people want to know and, in this book, I endeavour to place it on record.

One thing keeps coming through to me loud and clear. It is that rose growing people, in the main, are delightful. I do not know whether it's that nice people grow roses or whether growing roses changes people's nature for the good, but it has been my joy over the years to meet people who are great folk and make my work as pleasant as I can wish for.

I am setting out to help you enjoy roses. Surely the job is almost done already for roses are, in themselves, a joy. It only remains now for me to smooth over some rough patches, sort out some misconceptions, suggest some more ways of enjoying roses and to introduce you to some different and interesting roses. You will then be well on the way to joining the ranks of true rose devotees.

Hybrid Spinosissima

'MERMAID'

CHAPTER ONE

Growing roses

Sun and shade, position, soil,
organic matter, compost, humus and loam

I would be stating the obvious to say that you grow roses so you can enjoy them. It is just as obvious that if you suffer backaches and scratches, and spend so much time on spraying and maintenance that you have none in which to enjoy your roses, you will wonder whether it is worth growing them.

I often shudder as I read how some experts recommend that you go about preparing, planting and caring for your roses. The body becomes weak at the thought of double trenching, soil supplements, routine spraying and painstaking pruning. Perhaps the expert is a successful exhibitor who is convinced that all of these measures are essential for the production of championship blooms (or perhaps he/she is looking for pity), but how many of us intend growing champion-ship blooms? My guess is that ninety-nine percent of us just want a steady display of colourful blooms commensurate with a moderate input of effort.

Roses are remarkably hardy and resilient, and will give fair results with almost total neglect. I do not suggest that you totally neglect your roses but, by observing some basic requirements, you can have a creditable display, and with a little more attention to detail you will be pleasantly surprised with the results.

I have assumed until now that the chores associated with growing roses are, indeed, chores. Perhaps your enjoyment comes from simply pottering around, pulling a weed here, snipping off a dead head there. I have often been asked, sometimes with a note of sarcasm, whether I believe in talking to my roses, whereupon I reply that I do, but not for the expected reason. Yes, go out and talk to your roses. It probably will not help them but, while talking, you will notice that they need watering, that there are a few aphids to knock off or some seed pods to cut off. So it should be with all of your rose maintenance. Treat it as therapy and pleasure just to potter around the roses, taking your time, taking in their beauty. Then the backaches and scratches will not seem nearly as bad.

Easy culture has two aspects: choosing the best varieties for the purpose and planting them in the best place in the garden. Let us look first at the important question of **where**.

As I have already said, roses are very hardy and easy to grow. If the conditions are less than ideal, you may have to accept something less than top performance, or you may have to be prepared to do a little extra to offset the particular problems.

Roses grow best in full sun, in a temperate climate, fairly well in the open, away from other robbing plants, in a soil that is sandy loam to clay loam with a pH value of 6 to 7.

You are fortunate indeed if you have such conditions, but do not be too worried if you do not, as small adjustments to your planning and routine can usually allow your roses to succeed regardless of an imperfect environment.

Sun and Shade

Roses will take all the sunlight that you can give them. Many home gardens are faced with the opposite — too much shade. The greater the shade, the fewer the blooms and the more leggy the growth.

Up to half the day in shade does not matter much, but performance drops away with any more. Shade filtered through trees will give you more chance of success than the solid shade cast by buildings or fences. Growing roses on the southern side of a house is particularly difficult because they are in shade during the winter months due to the low angle of the sun and as the hot summer sun rises to nearly vertical it bears down on the previously protected soft plants, with the possibility of burning them severely. In a similar way, an area which receives a short burst of direct sun in mid-afternoon, say through a gap in the trees or between the roof and the fence, is also liable to sunburn.

The reflected heat from walls and fences also needs to be watched. Contrary to what people often imagine, reflected heat from a north wall is not great for the summer sun is almost overhead. However, watch out when planting against a west-facing wall or fence. New corrugated iron reflects heat like a furnace, and white-painted or plastered walls and fences are also a danger. Painting the corrugated iron a dark colour, such as olive or beige, not only reduces the reflected heat but also looks infinitely more suited to a garden setting.

If you expect a problem with sunburn, be sure that you do not let the roses become dry and stop growing. Never let the leaves fall because of dryness or disease, as the exposed branches will almost certainly scald badly.

Position

Roses like an open position which exposes them to the normal winds and breezes. They are remarkably hardy and tolerant of strong winds, but the blooms may become damaged by constant battering. Therefore, it is advisable to avoid growing tall roses but to plant low-to-medium height varieties in compact, block-shaped beds so that they protect each other against the winds.

Try to avoid planting in draughty tunnels such as between a house and nearby fence in a position that receives the prevailing winds, or near a corner which catches the cold wind as it whips around. In these conditions roses survive but never seem to flourish. It helps considerably to erect suitably placed screens of wind-break or shade cloth on the windward side. As you no doubt appreciate, you cannot stop the wind with a solid fence, for the wind will only swirl around further on, with more ferocity. A better arrangement is an open screen, such as wind-break cloth, or pickets giving about fifty percent protection which merely slows the wind down to a tolerable level.

In contrast to the too-windy situation, rose gardens which are completely protected from the wind can suffer from fungus problems, especially powdery mildew. Often you cannot do much about existing locations, other than to be prepared to spray often for fungus diseases, but if you can allow a certain amount of filtered wind through the garden, so much the better.

I have sometimes been asked whether rose roots interfere with sewer pipes and building foundations. Roses are not large shrubs and have fairly fine, fibrous roots, so I would be surprised if they cause any problems in that area.

Soil

Soil is inherited with a block of land. It is also one of the most important components for easy rose growing. There is nevertheless a lot that you can do to prepare your soil for a rose garden, and to ensure that its quality improves. Soil of any kind is not an inert, static substance; it is a living structure, teeming with micro-organisms that are interacting with the plants living in it. This may sound very daunting but as natural forces tend to keep the soil in balance under most circumstances, there is usally not much to worry about. It is only when soil is consistently too wet or too dry, over-fertilized, over-cultivated, over-cleared or poisoned in some way that the natural structure is spoiled. A good soil is self-generating. Given adequate water, the canopy of foliage is constantly falling onto the ground and slowly decomposing while it acts as a soil mulch. The dead foliage is gradually incorporated into the soil as humus, which improves the soil so that subsequent plant growth is better, thus adding more leaf mulch to the soil, and so on. Out of sight, underground, the network of roots is becoming thicker and thicker, which in turn helps to improve the soil structure.

When looking round the garden for somewhere to plant your roses, leaving aside landscaping considerations, look for the following:

Nearby trees and shrubs

Tree and shrub roots which rob the rose roots of moisture are among the most prevalent causes of poor performance, especially in dry climates. It is even more difficult if your roses are the only plants to be watered, because the tree roots will grow into their area and take the largest share of the available moisture. Digging a deep trench in order to hinder the invading roots will provide only a temporary reprieve, and lining the trench with a plastic film will only hold the roots at bay a little longer but this must be repeated every one or two years to be of any real benefit.

Drainage

The need for good drainage figures prominently in overseas literature and, indeed, there are areas in Australia and New Zealand where poorly draining soils can be a problem, but there are as many areas where roses can take all the water that they can get and love it. It is not possible to generalize about the need for special drainage works, for such factors as soil structure, subsoil, neighbouring run-off and subsoil seepage all play a part in determining drainage requirements. During winter, dig holes in suspect places in the garden to spade depth or 300 mm, fill with water several times and note how quickly they drain. Holes which retain water for one or two days suggest that special grading or agricultural drains are required. Simply raising the rose bed by 50–100 mm is often adequate in marginally wet areas.

Dry areas

Growing roses in dry areas is not difficult. In order to conserve precious water, the rose beds should be slightly sunken so that they may be flood irrigated instead of being watered by overhead sprinklers. A heavy layer of mulch on the ground is also vital.

Soil types

Roses will grow well in a wide range of soil types. They appreciate a high level of organic material but not to the extreme where the soil lacks the ability to hold a plant firmly in the ground. Sandy to heavy loams are quite suitable, as long as the sandy loam retains enough moisture and the heavy loam has adequate drainage. Limestone subsoils do not pose a problem provided that you do not activate the limestone by trying to dig through the limestone layer or mixing it in with the top soil. If you must puncture the limestone crust to improve the drainage, remove as much of the free limestone as is practicable.

Soil pH

The relative acidity or alkalinity of the soil determines which elements of food are available to a plant, and thus its resultant vigour. Roses seem to prefer a slightly acid soil with a pH value of from pH 6 to 7 (neutral) for best results. See page 25 for more information.

I hope that I have given you some ideas for planning your rose planting and I hope that I have not demolished too many other plans. It is best to know what difficulties might lie ahead so that you can overcome or skirt around them.

It remains now for you to prepare the soil for planting.

First, look at the history and present condition of the soil.

Is it a jungle of weeds? If so, the soil is fertile which, of course, is good news.

Knock the weeds down with a glyphosate weedicide (Zero, Roundup, V-7, Comkil). This will eliminate all weeds including couch, kikuyu and other persistent rhizome weeds and, more importantly, it will not poison the soil.

If it has been a barren path or driveway, or a much-trampled building site, that is not so good. If you have sufficient time, grow an annual crop of flowers or vegetables on the site, working in plenty of compost or about 50 mm of peat moss or other soil conditioner for as long a period as possible before planting.

If it has been just another part of the garden, from which you have perhaps taken out a large tree or reclaimed some lawn, this is not usually a problem. You will generally find that the soil is nice and friable from the roots and leaf compost of the previous plants. Fork over the ground deeply, removing any large tree roots that you find. If there is a large hole left after removing a tree, refill and flood the hole a couple of times to ensure that is does not continue to subside. Again, a quick crop of annuals or vegetables will help to settle the ground and show up any problems that might be there.

If it has been a former rose garden, **beware**. This is one of the most frequent reasons for a new rose bed to fail. Gardeners used to say that the soil was ''rose sick''. Recent opinion suggests that the decaying roots of the former roses produce a toxin that suppresses the new plants. Whatever the reason, the fact is that if you dig out a rose and immediately plant a new one in its place, the new plant will barely move. It probably will not die but will take two or three years to grow to anywhere near the size you would expect of a new plant. The bigger the original plant, the greater the problem seems to be for the new hopeful.

There are three ways to get around the problem.

Soil replacement. Cart away the soil from the immediate vicinity of the old rose and replace it with fresh soil. By all means use the old rose soil elsewhere in the garden. Any non-rose soil that can be scrounged around the garden is fine for the replacement soil. Replace a full barrow load for each average-sized plant; more for a large bush or climber.

Soil resting. You can grow a short-term crop in the old rose bed, preferrably one which involves turning and feeding the soil consistently. The bed should be ready for replanting with roses in one to two years.

Soil fumigation. A quick and effective method is to have the rose-bed area professionally gassed with methyl bromide, a total soil sterilizer. Obviously. this involves additional cost, and there is a slight risk that nearby roots passing under the bed may be poisoned, thus mildly damaging such trees or plants.

Filling Soil

Up to this stage I have assumed that you have a nicely graded garden area and that the roses are to be planted straight into the ground at its natural level. Unfortunately, that is not always the case. For a number of very good reasons you may have to change the level of the rose bed. Perhaps the natural soil has been bulldozed away during building or perhaps you want to raise the bed level to create additional drainage.

15

In all such cases you will be looking for some additional soil, and it is here that I sound a note of caution. Good garden loam is at a premium, especially in large cities. You usually get what you pay for but, especially if the soil appears to be a bargain, be sure that it does not carry noxious weeds, is not salt laden or so devoid of organic matter that it sets like concrete.

There are a few ways in which you can reduce your dependence on commercial garden loam.

If you are building, have the contractor stockpile the top soil from under the foundations and driveways, for future use in the garden.

Be on the lookout for anyone else who is building and has not the foresight or need to save their top soil. You may be able to arrange a deal.

If your soil is fairly heavy, and would benefit from the addition of a lighter component, use good, clean beach sand instead of loam. It is cheaper and safer.

Do not use expensive loam to fill too deeply. Try wherever possible to have your natural soil graded to an approximate level first, then add an even layer of loam on top to no more than 100–150 mm. Follow this with a scarifying or deep forking so that your original soil is partially mixed with the imported soil. There are two good reasons for this. Firstly, distinct strata of dissimilar soils cause all kinds of watering and drainage problems; and secondly, as you may be aware, it is only about the top 150 mm of soil which is alive with the micro-organisms that are so essential for good plant growth. Imported loam has usually been dug out from much greater depths and is consequently "dead". The reintroduction of your top soil quite literally inoculates the new soil with these micro-organisms.

Organic Matter, Mulch, Compost, Humus and Loam

All of these terms occupy a sort of grey area in the understanding of many new gardeners. They are all related to soil composition in some way.

Organic matter is any sort of vegetable or animal material, be it leaves, stems, bark or roots, or processed material such as paper, cardboard or sawdust and shavings. It is capable of decomposing in the elements. A garden **mulch** is often organic and, apart from performing its duty as a mulch, it gradually decomposes into the soil. **Compost** is organic matter that has partially broken down into a friable consistency. **Humus** is the final, almost permanent residue of organic matter in the soil. It converts hard barren soil into friable **loam**.

The amount of organic matter in the soil determines the way in which your roses will grow. You can prepare and cultivate a loamy soil easily and well, and the roots can penetrate it freely. Just as importantly, the organic matter acts like a

---

(Top)   SWEET HOME Suited both for massed planting and for cutting shapely blooms for floral decorations.

(Centre left)   OLD MASTER The breeder, Sam McGredy, calls this a 'Hand painted' effect. This is a trend that is bound to continue and develop.

(Centre right) LILAC CHARM Another lowish border rose featuring the particular charm of the simple five petalled roses.

(Bottom)   FRIESIA Intensely bright greenish yellow and a distinctive fragrance.

reservoir and converter for the water and nutrients which the roses need. The roses will benefit from a good level of organic matter at planting time, but there should also be a constant supply of mulch and leaves decomposing in the soil.

But, like all good things, even organics can be overdone, for roses like to be held firmly in the soil so that they do not move in the wind. Loamy soil, yes, but with sufficient body to hold the plant firmly.

The final preparation for planting should go something like this:

Make an assessment of the organic content of the soil (good, average or poor).

Add a layer of compost about 25 mm to 75 mm thick, depending on the need of the soil, and fork this deeply and thoroughly into the soil to the depth of the tines.

Prepare an area of between 700 mm^2 and 1 m^2 per plant (except when planting miniatures, which need only about 400 mm^2).

If you do not have access to good compost, partly rotted stable manure, sheep manure or cowpats are suitable, provided that they have weathered sufficiently to lose their burn. Be especially cautious when applying bird (poultry) manures as they are very concentrated when fresh. If the soil is of good texture but you have none of the mentioned materials available, a dressing of blood and bone is helpful. Heavy, sticky soils are improved by a liberal dressing of gypsum. Although it has no nutritional value, it is safe to use and makes the soil distinctly more friable and easier to work.

All of these preparations should ideally be done one or two months before planting, to let the soil settle to its final level and to allow any signs of freshness to leach out of the manures or fertilizers.

Finally, I stress an approach of moderation. I am sure that just as many roses are killed by too much attention as die through neglect.

(Top left) MABELLA Arriving without the usual fanfares, 'Mabella' is steadily becoming one of the leading yellows.

(Top right) MANOU MEILLAND Overseas trial gardens ranked this amongst the best ever. Its performance in the southern hemisphere support that claim.

(Centre left) HARRY WHEATCROFT Striped roses have often proved to be unstable. This is a completely satisfactory and attractive variety for this effect.

(Centre right) APRICOT NECTAR With soft apricot blooms and light matt foliage the effect is one of subtle beauty.

(Bottom left) JUST JOEY An English term for cute endearment, the rippling petals and distinctive colour make it instantly appealing.

(Bottom right) GOLD BUNNY For sheer volume of blooms and sustained flowering this is hard to beat, and each of the blooms are delightfully formed.

19

CHAPTER TWO

Easy care of your roses

Mulching, watering, cultivation, fertilizing

Choosing and buying roses is surely one activity which brings about family involvement more than almost anything else. At least that is the impression that I get from the families that pass through our nursery.

Husband, wife, children and often some in-laws arrive, always in the most leisurely manner, and spend the next one or two hours or half a day exploring every nook and cranny of the gardens, pouring out a "cuppa" by the creek and, finally, coming inside to place their order. Rose growers are friendly people, and there is always a lot of banter about their choices and who wants what and who is going to do what. Coming through all of this chit-chat is a common thread — once the roses have been chosen, they have to be maintained. Sometimes, even while an order is being placed, I can hear rumblings about pruning, spraying, weeding and watering — work, work, work.

I suggest that with rose growing you can apply the rule of diminishing returns. Simply, it takes a certain amount of effort to produce a perfect rose or a perfect display of roses, but the results will be nearly as good with only half as much time and effort; and with virtually no maintenance at all, in a temperate climate, you can have a passable display. It is up to you to decide how much attention you want to give your roses in return for a certain standard of display. In this section on maintenance, which I prefer to call "easy care", I shall give you the option of various standards of care from the laissez-faire to the perfectionist. In general, the emphasis is on the easiest, most practical method.

Mulching

Mulching is the practice of covering the soil with a heavy layer of material, either organic or inorganic, to help to retain moisture and smother weeds. As far as roses are concerned, mulching constitutes the biggest single easy care programme. It has

20

come increasingly into favour with Australians since they have become more aware that their gardens lack two vital compenents that are lacking in our harsh environment — water and organic matter. To a large degree, mulching helps to provide them. It is really only an adoption from nature of the continual shedding of mulch-forming leaves and twigs in the scrub or forest. This means that leaves, twigs and bark are highly suitable mulching materials. But the list is much greater: meadow hay, pea straw, seaweed, wood chips, shavings, old animal manures and some residues from processing such as rice hulls, grape marc and fruit and nut shells are all useful, and thick layers of newspaper, old carpet underfelt and thick jute bags can be pressed into service too. A few inorganic materials such as scoria, smooth pebbles, crushed clay tiles and black plastic may be used but, although they conserve moisture, they do not provide a continual supply of humus for the soil as an organic, slowly rotting mulch.

Spread your mulch generously all through the rose beds, as wide as the branch-spread of the bushes, which is usually about 1 m across. It should be thick enough to completely cover and seal the ground. A thick material such as wood chips would need to be 50 mm thick, while a more open material such as straw or grass should be 70–100 mm to adequately seal the area.

Renew or top up the mulch at the end of each wet season so that your roses benefit from the thicker mulch for the coming dry weather.

There are just a few problems that you should be alerted to with some mulches:

- Rapidly decaying materials, such as lawn clippings may create a nitrogen deficiency which can best be corrected with a dressing of blood and bone.
- Fresh lawn clippings may generate heat as they ferment, thus burning the crown of the rose, so keep them clear of the actual plant.
- Fine material such as sawdust can become so tightly packed that it becomes waterproof, so it should be scarified from time to time.
- Sheep manure, although a good rich fertilizer, carries a lot of weed seeds.
- Most mulches, unfortunately, provide a harbour for spores and eggs of pests and diseases, so be sure to thoroughly spray the mulch when doing your routine winter spraying.
- Birds love to scratch amongst the mulch and can leave it scattered in all directions, but this is scarcely a problem if you enjoy the company of birds and other benefits that they bring.

Surprisingly, seaweed does not contain much free salt so, after a brief rinse before putting it down, it is one of the best materials.

Watering

Watering plays a very important part in growing roses in harsh climates — not because of the quantity of water that roses need but because they must have it applied properly.

Roses are moderately deep-rooted plants if they have been trained correctly, and their watering requirements are simple. A deep flooding equivalent to 30–40 mm of rain each fortnight in the spring and autumn and weekly in hot weather is plenty, provided of course that rain has not fallen. Quick-draining sandy soils need to be watered two or three times more frequently with the equivalent of 20–30 mm of rain. So far so good, for these deep waterings have encouraged the rose roots to seek water from deep down and, in the case of, for example, your taking an extended holiday away, your roses will come through without distress.

Problems arise when you have a mixed garden of roses, annuals, lawn and shrubs, which is a common combination, because lawn and annuals need only a light watering about twice a week. If you assume that your lawn watering is sufficient for the roses nearby and that they are receiving the overflow, you will have trouble. In this situation rose roots develop near the surface of the soil, for that is the only damp area, and before you realize it they will look distinctly unfruitful, being the loser in the contest for moisture against the shallow-rooting lawn. In addition, the continual light waterings are an open invitation for black spot disease on the leaves, and salt damage if the salinity in the water is high.

Unfortunately, the sudden increase in completely automatic watering systems has brought some problems too. An automatic system in itself is not necessarily at fault, but some of the equipment salesmen seem to be more accomplished at making a sale than they are at designing a system that suits the whole garden. The main purpose of the systems is to relieve the gardener of the chore of frequent lawn waterings, but it is so easy to go ahead and install a system throughout the whole garden, overlooking the differing needs of each group of plants. I cannot give you an all-embracing answer to the problem, but can offer these suggestions which you should try to incorporate in your watering programme:

- Water below the foliage when practical, especially during hot days.

- Use drip or trickle irrigation. As the plants become larger, move the emitters to a point midway between each plant to spread the roots wider. Run the system for 12 to 24 hours at each application.

- Half-way border jets arranged around the edge of the rose bed and throwing low under the foliage are cheap and effective.

- Roses are rather sensitive to saline water. They start to show damage when salinity exceeds 600 to 800 p.p.m. (parts per million) in overhead watering. Salinity of up to 1500 p.p.m. can be tolerated when flooding or drip irrigation is used, but be sure that the soil is well drained, and keep up regular floodings to wash the residual salt away from the root zone.

- Save the summer showers (a handy hint). Many metropolitan gardens have their roof water piped direct into the street. This is fine for ridding the garden of surplus water, but wastes the welcome summer showers when the garden is parched. Have a deflector fitted to your downpipes so that the water spills out onto the garden when needed. Remove the deflector when the garden has had sufficient.

Cultivation

We cultivate the soil to prepare it for planting, to control weeds and to prevent water losses from its surface.

Supposing that your roses are already planted, and your mulch has smothered the weeds and is preventing the soil from drying out, I leave it to you to decide whether the soil needs cultivating.

In practice, you will find that a few weeds penetrate the mulch. Some can easily be pulled by hand but, if this is not practical, a simple torpedo hoe makes light work of them as its double-edged blade reaches under the branches and slides beneath the mulch, scarcely disrupting it. More persistent weeds (usually rhizome types such as couch, kikuyu and convolvulus) are easily killed by the glyphosate weed sprays which are sold under several commercial names. Fortunately, roses are fairly tolerant of glyphosate, although you should avoid direct contact and immediately wash off any that drifts onto the rose leaves.

Finally, healthy loamy soil is a teeming colony of all manner of soil organisms, each doing their particular function in a delicately balanced ecosystem. Not the least of these are the earthworms who love to move between the soil and the surface mulch, steadily decomposing the mulch and leaving burrows and trails of casts which do far more to loosen the soil than any cultivation will ever do.

Fertilizing

Chemical companies urge you to use their complete rose manures while environmentalists tell you that natural organic manures are the best thing and that chemicals poison the soil. Little wonder if you are confused.

Organic matter consists of many things including weeds, roots, leaves, animal droppings, chicken litter, vegetables, fruit, paper and sawdust. When any or all of these waste products are turned into the soil, or when they are incorporated into a compost heap, they start to decompose, returning a large amount of the nutrient needs of the living plants and improving the structure of the soil. In addition, the organic matter in the soil acts as a benign buffer. It retains moisture without making the soil cold and waterlogged, it creates the air spaces that are essential if the soil is to breathe and it acts as a holder and converter of the chemical fertilizers that may be added. Small wonder that many people are unashamed enthusiasts of organic gardening. If we could incorporate enough organic material into our soils (especially sandy soils and difficult, sticky, black or yellow clays), we would scarcely have to use artificial fertilizers. In practice, we can seldom achieve this, so we add occasional boosters of manufactured fertilizers to supplement the natural nutrients. Any rose manure of reputable brand may be used. It should contain an appropriate balance between nitrogen (N), potassium (P) and phosphorus (K), and the addition of minor and trace elements at least every year or two is recommended.

A word of warning! If X amount of fertilizer gives a certain plant response, do not assume that twice-X will give double the response, because it will not. The amount recommended should give you the optimum growth. Additional amounts will only increase the salinity of the soil (fertilizers are forms of salts) and will most likely burn the roots and retard the growth.

In summary, your feeding programme should consist of:

the addition of up to 50 mm of compost or fine organic material at planting;

the application of a steadily decomposing mulch (50–100 mm deep) each year;

three boosters of rose manure each year — a medium handful at pruning time (winter) and somewhat less, say a small handful, after spring flowering and again in February when preparing for the autumn display.

One technique which will give you a longer-term supply is called core feeding. Instead of sprinkling the fertilizer around the plant and lightly scratching it in, press holes (about 200–300 mm deep) in the ground between each plant with a crowbar or thick spike, and fill the holes with fertilizer. The core of feed attracts the roots so that far less is lost through leaching and, because there are only one or two deposits around each plant, the chances of manure-burn are far less.

Slow-release fertilizers are also ideal for roses, especially at planting time. Use one of the long-term formulations. Foliage fertilizers are useful if you want to give your roses a boost for a special occasion but they are not recommended for general purposes.

Young plants that are not getting away to a good start seldom need fertilizer to help them. In fact, if they have not achieved much root development, an over-zealous dressing of feed will do more harm than good. In cases of poor early growth, look for causes such as waterlogging, the presence of toxic substances in the soil (e.g. lime or weed spray) or heavy deprivation of soil nutrients and water by nearby trees.

The colour and pattern of the leaves of a rose can tell you a lot about its requirements. Feed deficiencies usually appear as fairly symmetrical patterns, whereas diseases (except virus mosaic) create a random, irregular pattern.

Nitrogen is the most dynamic of plant foods. In abundance it causes plants to make rapid leafy, soft growth; its deficiency causes the growing tips to become small and butter-yellow, with stunted growth and premature leaf drop. Large amounts of rotting straw or woody materials in the soil deprive the plants of nitrogen but, when the decomposition has finished, the balance is usually restored. Small but regular dressings of blood and bone, sulphate of ammonia, urea, or bird (poultry) manure will help. Thunder showers also wash nitrogen from the air. Too heavy applications of nitrogen can cause root burn, so use with caution and stop as soon as the colour is restored to the leaves. Excessive nitrogen will give lovely-looking growth, but it will be soft and succulent, thus very prone to disease and insect attack, and damage by wind, hail, frost and the like.

Phosphorus is important for maturing the plant growth and in the production of flowers and fruit. It is generally deficient in Australian soils but normal dressings of an N.P.K. fertilizer will provide the needs of the plant for a year or two. Symptoms of a deficiency are not obvious; merely a purplish blotchiness against rather deepish-green leaves.

Potassium, the third of the major elements, is important in balancing the soft growth stimulated by nitrogen and aids in the production of plant starches. It is usually readily available in heavy soils but leaches from fast-draining soils, where its deficiency can be seen as a reddish margin around the tips and edges of the leaves. Again, a balanced N.P.K. fertilizer should be sufficient but, for a specific supplement, add it in the form of sulphate of potash.

Iron (Fe) and **manganese** (Mn) are the other elements that sometimes need special attention. Both become ''locked up'' in alkaline or limestone soils, in which case both show up as yellow veining of the leaves. Iron deficiency shows on the young growth as yellow leaves with only the veins remaining green. The addition of iron chelate, which is a form of iron not locked up by limestone, will give rapid results.

Manganese deficiency shows on the older leaves as areas of yellow around the edges and in the areas between the veins. A small teaspoonful (5–6 mg per m^2) of manganese sulphate applied to each plant should remedy the problem.

Acidity and Alkalinity of the Soil
(pH value — pH 7.0 = neutral)
Roses respond best when the soil is slightly acid (from pH 6.0 to 7.0) but will give fair results in soils ranging half a point either side (pH 5.5 to 7.5). Outside these limits certain elements become deficient, e.g. iron and manganese in alkaline soils, and magnesium in acid soils. You can obtain pH tests of your soil from State botanic gardens, departments of agriculture and some private firms.

The C.S.I.R.O. has developed a simple colour-reaction kit which is marketed by Hortico and which is an adequate guide for most home gardeners. In general, it is better to try to bring your soil to ideal acidity than to be constantly adding elements to rectify problems. Dressings of agricultural sulphur will bring the soil towards acidity (lower the pH number) and, if your soil is too acid, the addition of garden lime will increase its alkalinity (raise the pH number).

Problems
Salty water (salinity) is an all too common problem in some parts of Australia and is likely to get worse as our water resources are pushed to their limit.

There are two aspects to the problem. The first is caused by the salty deposit that forms on the leaves following sprinkling with fine sprinklers during hot weather. This occurs when the salinity exceeds about 600 parts per million. The leaves will look dry and salt encrusted, with dead margins.

The other aspect of salinity concerns soil moisture, which is the actual water that is available for the plant to ''drink'' through its roots. When water is applied direct to the ground by flooding or drip irrigation, and you are able to leach the salt away from the root zone by occasional heavy floodings, then the rose will tolerate salinity up to 1200–1500 p.p.m. Should the leaves become limp and light-brown with considerable marginal drying, then this salinity level has probably been exceeded.

Weed sprays can seriously damage or kill roses. The most common weed spray in use today is probably glyphosate and, although roses are fairly tolerant, they can be damaged for a long period (1 to 2 years) if sprayed. Symptoms are distinct yellowing of the foliage, while the leaves become small and elongated.

Hormone weed sprays (e.g. 24D and 245T) cause grotesque new growth with thin twisted leaves and distorted buds, and sure death in extreme cases.

Soil-poison weedicides usually cause yellowing of the foliage, and if this occurs on only one part of the plant, the root zone serving that part of the rose has probably been affected. There is little that you an do about most accidental weed spray damage, other than wait for the effects to wear off. This can take as long as one or two years.

Sunburn can cause damage at times. A healthy rose carrying plenty of foliage is safe but, if it becomes denuded by disease, neglect or dryness, the stems facing directly towards the sun can be scalded right through the bark. The branches of bush roses can be trimmed back to form a new frame for the bush, but the stem of a stem rose or a weeper is a permanent part of the plant, so damage here could easily ruin the whole rose. Placing the supporting stake on the north-west side of the stem can create worthwhile shade.

Balling of rose blooms can be a nuisance. Roses with a mass of thin petals are very prone to ''balling'' in wet or dewy weather when the moisture sticks the petals together, preventing them from opening. They finally break down with mould. There is very little you can do about this other than select varieties with heavy petals and a more open form. Be guided by the best-performing varieties in your area.

Blind shoots, where the branch of a bush rose runs into a blind or flowerless tip, cause a lot of disappointment to some growers. It is a problem that has baffled the rose-growing fraternity for years, and many theories have been proposed. I think that there is no single cause. Some varieties seem to have a weakness in this direction; fertilizer imbalance, damage by insects at an early stage and weather conditions are possible causes but it seems that there is not much that most growers can do about the problem.

CHAPTER THREE

Pests and diseases

Aphids, two-spotted mite, thrips, caterpillars, scale

Black Spot, Powdery Mildew, rust, viruses

There are times when we should wait no longer for natural forces to cure an ailing rose and must intervene with a little help to tip the balance against the problem.

Practically all of the problems that affect roses are seasonal and climatic. This means that we know when to expect a certain problem to crop up and, similarly, when the conditions are right for it to be controlled naturally without help. Also certain varieties of roses are naturally more resistant or immune than others to pests and diseases. When considering pest and disease control we should first judge whether the problem is sufficiently bad to need treatment.

Consider treating your roses when the damage being done is worse than the phytotoxic damage which always affects plants to some degree when sprayed or treated with any chemicals, or is more than the cost and effort of the treatment.

Some people will argue that if a rose, or any plant for that matter, is growing in well-balanced soil in an ideal location it will not be bothered by pests and diseases. It is true that plants in ideal conditions have more natural resistance to the common ailments, but in practice conditions such as weather and soil are difficult to control, so we are still left with the need to administer some additional help.

Pests

Pests are usually considered to be the insects, and we will look at them in their approximate order of importance.

Aphids (sometimes called *greenfly*) are soft, "juicy" insects of 1–2 mm long. They are usually green, but sometimes light-brown, and sometimes winged. They feed on the soft tips and buds of the roses. They are most active in the spring and autumn when they multiply at a prodigious rate. A colony may completely cover the tip of growth for 60–80 mm, feeding on the sap of the plant through their fine proboscis. In such quantities, they can seriously retard the plant and ruin the blooms. They are especially damaging to the new shoots of only about 10 mm long, for the emerging leaves become malformed with much the same appearance as "curl-leaf" in peaches.

Several degrees of treatment are available.

1. The early massed colony may be broken up and washed away by jetting with a hose or dousing with water. Doing this a few times will give the aphids' natural predators (lacewings, hoverflies, ladybirds and some small birds) time to build up.
2. When the infestation is more general, a pyrethrum spray is safe and moderately successful. Malathion will wipe out the infestation for a week or two but it kills all other insects as well.
3. For complete, long-lasting control, you will have to resort to a light spraying of Metasystox or Rogor 40, which enter the plant's system and continue to kill all sucking insects for from four to six weeks. Use both chemicals with great care. Do not be too concerned if occasional aphids escape the sprays for they will be controlled by predators who will find them a stimulus to stay close at hand for another outbreak.
4. For many years garlic has been claimed to suppress aphids. Recent research has proved this to be a fact and, as a result, garlic sprays are now coming onto the market.

Two-spotted Mites (or *Spider-mites* or *Red spiders*) are one of the most difficult insects to detect and one of the trickiest to control. They occur in hot, dry conditions where they quickly build up to plague proportions on the undersides of older leaves. The foliage in general looks dry, as if in need of watering, and on looking at the backs of the leaves, you will see pockets of fine web. On closer examination, particularly with a magnifying glass, you will see masses of fat, light, amber-coloured mites, and eggs almost the size of the insects. They are sucking insects which effectively bring the plant to a standstill and cause leaf drop.

These mites are retarded by regular spraying of the undersides of the leaves with water. They also dislike sulphur dust and Benlate spray, but for thorough eradication you must use a systemic insecticide such as Kelthane or Metasystox. The mites are quick to develop resistance to certain sprays, so change your spray from time to time. The ideal solution is the introduction of predator mites. This technique is in use commercially and, no doubt, a domestic service is not far away.

Thrips are the same insects that play havoc with the blooms of fruit trees in the spring. They are slim-winged insects of only 1 mm in length, and they look more like slivers of black wood than insects as they nestle inside the petals of the blooms. They especially prefer light-coloured blooms, and leave them looking bruised and lustreless.

Thrips appear within a few hours, often blown by a warm north wind, and sometimes disappear as quickly as they arrive. Because of this, together with the fact that they are hard to control for long periods, it is sometimes easiest to let the roses take their chances without treatment. If you need a clean display for a special

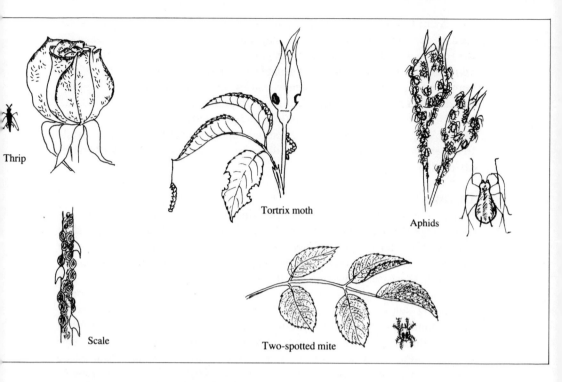

Thrip

Tortrix moth

Aphids

Scale

Two-spotted mite

occasion, resort to spraying with Orthene.

Caterpillars of a few types damage roses. The worst is the tortryx moth caterpillar which appears in the spring. Should you see small, light-grey moths near the roses, look for the caterpillars. They are green, up to 15 mm long, and can be found either boring through the rose-buds or drawing folds of leaves around themselves. Consequently, they are not easily noticed. When your blooms open peppered with fine holes, you realize that the damage has been done. When disturbed, caterpillars move quickly, often dropping to the ground by a thread.

Caterpillars of all types are safely controlled with Dipel, a specific caterpillar stomach poison which is harmless to other forms of animal life, or with Carbaryl which is rather more toxic.

Circulio Beetles can be damaging, especially in dry conditions. The steel grey-black beetles are under 10 mm in length. They chew a saw-tooth pattern into the lower leaves and axil buds. You see the result rather than the beetle, for it hides during the day in the loose dry soil at the base of the plant and, if found by carefully exploring in this area, behaves as if dead. If the beetles are causing too much damage, spray the lower foliage with dieldrin or lead arsenate.

Scale occasionally affect roses. They are insects which fix themselves to the older stems of the plant, under the protection of a waxy shield. A spray of half-strength Malathion and half-strength white oil should be sufficient to keep them in check.

29

Nematodes (or *Eelworms*) are microscopic worms of various types which feed on the roots of host plants, causing varying degrees of damage. Generally they can be identified only by laboratory examination so, if all other measures fail, you will have to seek the help of a suitable government or private laboratory. One common type, the rootknot nematode, causes small lesions with clustering roots which give a good clue to identification of the problem.

Nematodes are more likely to occur in light sandy soils than in heavy soils. Marigolds growing in the soil have a strong suppressing effect on the pest, while treatment with Nemagard is a more direct (if not as environmentally desirable) alternative.

Diseases

Fungal diseases on roses are largely determined by weather conditions, so you can often judge the likelihood of a problem curing itself or continuing and spreading because of the prevailing conditions. Remember that a bad infestation, say at the end of a season, can produce a mass of spores ready to start an infestation next season. In this case, prevention is better than cure.

Fungicides in general are not too damaging to the environment. Treatments containing sulphur and copper can be mildly beneficial, but repeated heavy applications of the newer systemic fungicides may eventually lead to a resistant strain of the fungus, so it is advisable to change your spray programme from time to time. Some roses are distinctly more resistant than others to certain fungal diseases so by all means spray only the affected roses rather than the whole garden.

Black Spot, as the name implies, is a random scattering of irregular, ragged blotches on the lower leaves, followed shortly by a yellowing of the remainder of the leaves, which then drop prematurely. Eventually, the whole plant may become denuded by a bad infestation, which leads to a weakening of the plant and an extraordinary number of branches which die back.

Black Spot thrives in high humidity and warmth, and is consequently the major problem on the east coast and in northern semi-tropical areas. The practice of overhead watering late in the day, which leaves the foliage wet for long periods, also encourages the disease. Spray at the first signs, or even at the onset of likely conditions, with Thiram (T.M.T.D.), Mancozeb (Diathane M45) or the systemic fungicide Triforine.

Powdery Mildew is also aptly named. The young soft leaves, stems and buds, and even the thorns at the top of the plant take on a blotchy white, powdery appearance followed by distinct distortion of the leaves and malformation of the buds. Mildew usually occurs in the spring and autumn in conditions of fine, mild days and dewy nights, although it can occur at almost any time of the year. Consequently, powdery mildew is one of the main worries of rose growers in western, southern and inland Australia.

Treatment traditionally has been by sulphur applied as a light dust when the temperature is over 25°C or sprayed as a "wettable" sulphur. In the cooler weather, spray the affected foliage with Karathane, Benlate or Triforine.

Rust is most damaging in the spring when small rusty-orange specks appear on the backs of the leaves, causing corresponding bright-green spots on the tops. The rest of the leaf turns yellow-brown. Leaves eventually drop off but by that time an extensive reservoir of spores has been produced for next year's infestation. Spray with Zineb or Triforine.

All of the sprays mentioned should be readily available in domestic packs. However, there are several new, extremely effective chemicals which are available only in large commercial packages. If you have a large area to spray it would be worth asking a specialist supplier or stock agent about these additional chemicals.

Wilt and Dieback is another disease of which you should be aware. Little is known about its exact nature and how it is spread but, while it is fatal, it is not prevalent enough to be a serious problem.

In the spring time, when the rose is making its most rapid growth, random branches take on a curious wilting appearance. The leaves reflex to form a characteristic balling appearance and turn light yellow; the stems taper to a blind tip, turning yellow and finally black as the leaves fall, and the texture of the stem becomes soft and brittle. Aphid damage to young shoots in the spring can look similar, but the leaf curl is not as balled and the stem does not develop the same yellowing and brittleness.

Later growth in the summer and autumn appears normal, leaving only the black, tapering dead branches as a clue to the existence of the disease. The following season more of the plant will die, until eventually it fails completely. We do not know how wilt and dieback spreads, so it is wise to dig out the offending plant immediately in case it transmits the disease to others. Do not try to propagate the plant from cuttings or buddings as these will most certainly fail in a short while.

Viruses occur from time to time, causing mosaic patterns on rose leaves and blemishes on petals. Some are unsightly, others are almost attractive and, in the main, they only slightly suppress the growth of the plant. They are permanently in the plant but are not easily transmitted to other roses, so it is safe to tolerate them in the garden.

Sprays and Sprayers

Although there are multi-purpose spray mixtures on the market, there is no doubt that despite their apparent convenience, specific sprays are more effective, and less harmful to the environment and the natural balance of predators in your garden.

Some sprays will mix together safely, and there are very comprehensive compatibility charts available from departments of agriculture and chemical firms. However, if you are not sure, *do not mix.*

Sprays, especially fungicides, lose their effectiveness with age, so keep only enough to last for about two or three years.

Some sprays are very toxic so always:

read and observe the directions on the packet;

31

wear protective gloves and mask, and long-sleeved, long-trousered clothes as circumstances warrant;

lock up your sprays and keep them well labelled and date marked.

Many types of sprayers are available. I suggest that you consider the following when deciding which to purchase.

- You will need 1 litre of spray for 3–6 plants.
- A spill-proof sprayer is safest.
- It should be capable of spraying upwards and downwards in order to cover all of the foliage when required.
- You get what you pay for. Cheap models are often made of unrepairable plastic (all plastic equipment should be kept out of direct sunlight when not in use).
- The "Little Boy" sprayer, which connects to the hose and mixes concentrate at the nozzle, is good value at low cost.
- A garden of over two hundred plants deserves a motorized sprayer, either a knapsack air-mister or a conventional power pump.

CHAPTER FOUR

Planting

Growing in containers, watering,
slow starters, support for climbers,
protection, recording and labelling.

The great moment has arrived! You have planned your garden, selected the plants and in due course you have received them. The ground has been prepared and has been lying roughly turned and waiting to accept its new tenants. You have a peg marking the place for each rose.

A lot has been said as to how to plant roses successfully. It would be too flippant for me to say that if you have good fresh plants and well prepared soil, you would only have to drop the plants into the ground and they would grow. But it would serve to make the point that rose planting is not difficult or mysterious.

When you receive your plants, be sure that they do not dry out. If the root wrapping still appears moist and well sealed, you can keep them in the cool for three or four days without unwrapping. If you cannot plant by then, they should be "heeled" into a trench of friable soil in the shade until required. Nevertheless the sooner you can plant them into their final home, the better, as they are set back each time they are uprooted.

Carry your new plants into the garden in a bucket of water. Armed with a sharp spade, dig holes about 200–300 mm wide and 200 mm deep. See that the bottom of the holes are well loosened, breaking any hard pans, and that any previously added organic matter is well rotted and mixed throughout the soil. Partly refill the hole with well broken soil to a depth where the plant will settle with the bud-union slightly (20–30 mm) above the ultimate ground level.

Some experts recommend planting the bud-union below the ground. This is not necessarily harmful, although as the years pass and the plant develops a large crown, and continual mulching raises the ground level, it becomes increasingly difficult to get at the crown to make a neat job when pruning.

It is worse to plant too high, exposing half or more of the rootstock, as this allows the plant to move around in the wind and prevents the roots from getting a

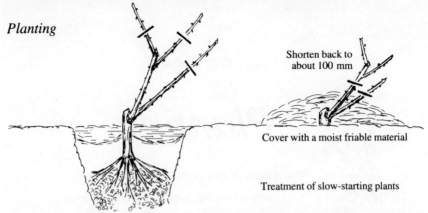

Shorten back to about 100 mm

Cover with a moist friable material

Treatment of slow-starting plants

good grip in the soil. Weeping roses and stem roses should have their roots planted about 100 mm below ground level.

It is not important which way the bud-union of the plant faces, but if it faces to the prevailing winds it may be less prone to damage in the early stages.

The roots should lie as naturally and untwisted as possible, and a small mound in the centre of the hole will hold up the conical spread of the roots. Refill the hole with well broken, friable soil and press down firmly with your foot. Fill the depression with water and allow to soak away a couple of times before finally raking the soil level all around.

It is risky and futile to add ordinary chemical fertilizers at planting. This should be delayed until after the first crop of flowers appears in about December. A small handful of slow-release fertilizer can, however, be safely scattered into the bottom of the hole.

As soon as the new buds start to swell, the new plants will benefit greatly by being pruned back to around four to six buds per branch. This has the effect of limiting the number of buds that the plant must feed and therefore producing better growth from near the base, which is where the new framework of the rose will emerge.

Roses growing in containers are planted out in much the same way. The rose is turned out of the container, the roots are lightly teased out without disturbing too much of the potting soil and planted to the same depth in relation to the bud-union.

Watering. The area around the new plant should be kept moist without being waterlogged. In winter the natural rains are usually sufficient but, when planting container-grown plants in summer, autumn or in periods of prolonged dryness, a weekly soaking is necessary.

Slow starters. Not all roses break dormancy at the same time, so do not be too worried if two or three weeks elapse between the first and last plants coming

---

(Top)   CHICAGO PEACE The best of several mutations that have come from 'Peace'.

(Centre left)   DUET Remarkably free flowering and hardy, it is a rose that gains your admiration the longer you grow it.

(Centre right)   SUSAN HAMPSHIRE Clusters of flowers are not necessarily small — eight huge blooms on this stem.

(Bottom)   PEACE (Mme. A. Meilland) The most famous and best known rose of all times. Introduced at the end of World War II (1945).

34

Rose rust

Powdery Mildew

Black S

3 examples of fungal diseases —

Saline-water

Water-logging

potash

2 examples of other leaf problems

Iron

manganese

phosphorus

5 examples of the effect of certain
deficiencies in the soil —

nitrogen

into leaf. If a new plant appears healthy but just will not start, try cutting the branches back quite hard, to about 70–100 mm, and covering the whole plant with a mound of friable, moist material such as compost, peat moss, old sawdust or lawn clippings. The moist, cool atmosphere thus created encourages new, strong shoots from the base in a very short time. Level out the mound when the plant is well on its way. Stem roses obviously cannot be covered in this way, but binding the stem and branches with straw, shredded paper or hessian, and keeping them regularly sprinkled with water often pulls them through.

Tall weeping roses need a firm stake or pipe for support at planting, as do 700 mm stem roses and mini-stems. It is best to set these in their holes before planting and drive them down until the top of the stake is about 100 mm above the bud-union. Tie the stems firmly to the stake with a material that will not cut or choke the bark and, more importantly, will not break in high winds. Two ties that I have used with good results are old pantyhose and malleable fencing wire threaded inside a short length of garden hose or trickle pipe.

Climbers need some means of support when they start making new canes sometime in the autumn after planting. There are a number of ways of providing them with the necessary trellis. Bearing in mind that they only require horizontal supports, the simplest trellis is a series of tightly stretched fencing wires 200–300 mm apart and 2–2.5 m high.

Bush roses do not need any form of support. During their first season, however, the plants are rather fragile, and easily fall victim to flying newspapers, careless feet and romping dogs. If you suspect that any such hazards could harm your roses, drive in two or three sticks wigwam-fashion over the plants. It will be well worth the trouble.

Recording and Labelling

You have finished planting and each plant should have a label attached so that you know exactly which rose is which. That will be just fine for about one year. Nursery labels do not last forever so, if you want to keep a permanent record, you must begin before it is too late.

First and foremost, keep a garden notebook, for all plants in the garden. You do not have to draw plans, but merely note, e.g., side fence, front to back — 'Europeana', 'Gold Bunny', 'Manou Meilland'. You might also note when and where you purchased each plant in case you ever need a replacement or an admiring friend wants one too.

Secondly, put your own labels on the plants. Galvanized iron sheet marked with a soft lead pencil, and thin metal tags (e.g. Permatags) embossed with a blunt point (such as a worn-out ballpoint pen) are both good, lasting labels. Pieces of venetian blind slat marked with Chinagraph or wax pencil last for several years, as do strips of wood painted with matt oil-based paint and marked with lead pencil. Ballpoint pen and most spirit pen markings will fade within a year or so.

Use scraps of insulated electrical cable or malleable wire for hanging the tags loosely onto the plants.

CHAPTER FIVE

Pruning

Why, when and how do we prune?

The annual winter chore of pruning seems to bother the new gardener (and many experienced ones too) more than any other aspect of rose growing. It is a daunting sight to approach a large prickly mass of twigs and know where to make the first secateur cut.

If you have read other books, seen pruning demonstrations or spoken with other gardeners, the chances are that each will tell you something different. On the surface this may sound very confusing, but when you stop to consider, it proves to you that there are few hard and fast rules for pruning, and that you have a wide range of techniques within which you can safely move.

Why Do We Prune?

- Pruning aims to anticipate the natural crowding of the branches which causes the older and more shaded ones to die out.
- Pruning keeps plants at a moderate size. Roses, if left to their own devices, gradually become larger and larger, and spill over into adjoining plants and paths.
- Pruning helps to produce the largest possible blooms by channelling the available resources into a few large stems instead of many smaller ones (if this is what you desire).
- If you live in an area where your roses are likely to be damaged by frost, they must be pruned down hard so that they can be covered as a protection against the frost.

It stands to reason that if you want a large, informal, minimum-maintenance display; if you do not require immaculately groomed plants; and if your roses are not affected by frosts, you do not need to prune at all. Many of the species and old-world roses, and some of the newer park-planting roses are at their best when unpruned. Sometimes it might be desirable to tidy up the plants, shortening long branches to encourage more compact flowering or to keep the overall size down a little, but such pruning consists merely of shaping with hedge shears or a motorized brush cutter.

I especially want to make the point that the style of pruning you choose will, to a large degree, determine the effect you receive from your roses. The general rule is that the more severe the pruning the larger and fewer the resultant blooms, and the lighter the pruning the greater the display of colour will be, but with reduced quality of blooms.

As a starting point, a pruned bush should be about half the height of the original plant, and the number of branches should be about half the original. The following year, you should observe the results to tell you if the pruning was too light or too severe to produce the effect that you wanted.

When Do We Prune?

The basic rule is that you prune after flowering. Because practically all modern roses flower continuously throughout spring, summer and autumn, pruning has to be done in winter, when the roses have reached their greatest point of dormancy. In warm climates they never actually stop growing, and you must seize your chance to prune during a pause; while in cool climates it is safe to prune when the axil buds start to swell. The axil bud is the ''eye'' that is tucked into the base of each leaf stem.

If you are in a frost prone area, do not be too anxious to start early, as the new growth that you stimulate may be damaged by late frosts.

The important exceptions to the ''prune in June'' rule are roses that flower only in spring, such as spring-flowering weeping roses, species roses (especially the well known Banksias) and the original old world roses. All of these are pruned in November or December. The winter-flowering Lorraine Lee is pruned in March for best results.

How Do We Prune?

A person who is well practised at pruning can set to work and cut away in what appears to be a completely random manner. To learn by watching them would be well nigh impossible but, despite the apparent lack of system, there are a number of definite things being done.

By considering the steps listed below, one by one in the first place it is easy to see what you are doing, and as your confidence and proficiency improve, you can run all of the steps together. These steps apply equally to all types of roses — bush roses, stem roses, miniatures and, to a large degree, climbers (see ''Pruning Climbers'', page 41).

Bear in mind that the small cluster roses (floribundas) and the stem roses are noted for their garden display, so prune on the light side, whereas the larger blooms (hybrid teas) must be pruned harder to encourage maximum-sized blooms. Miniatures are often so small that it is not practical to individually cut each stem, so a general thinning and shortening (sometimes referred to as a "short back and sides") is sufficient.

You may have been advised to shape a rose bush like a vase or inverted cone. Basically, this is good advice, but I think that it is far more important to prune your bushes to the best, most prominent and plump eyes carried on the young stout branches than to stick slavishly to the vase shape. It is all very well to cut the branches out of the centre to let the light in, but it is stupid to cut out a good branch from the centre if you are left with nothing suitable to make up the vase shape.

Do not worry about whether some branches are higher than others. Again, it is more important to cut to the best eye, regardless of its height, and it is better to cut down a poor branch than to leave it high but unproductive. If the plant looks irregular when you have finished, but you are confident that you have selected the best eyes, do not worry. The spring growth will soon cover the irregularities.

Before starting, arm yourself with a good-quality pair of sharp secateurs of the hook and blade type; a pruning saw, which will enable you to make a thorough job of the tough old branches near the crown of the plant; a pair of double-handed hook and blade shears to help make light work of the heavy branches; and a pair of leather gloves (or at least one on your non-cutting hand to make the job quicker and more comfortable). Carry a jar of the common household bleach, sodium hypochlorite, to sterilize the secateurs before you move onto the next plant.

Step 1. Cut out completely and neatly any dead or obviously sickly branches.

Step 2. Cut back any unproductive shoots, for example, any shoots that have not produced good flowering stems lately, especially if they are close to more productive braches.

Step 3. Cut out any branches that are crowded near, or crossing over, other good branches.

Step 4. Cut out or shorten any thin (say, less than the thickness of a pencil) twiggy shoots.

Step 5. Shorten the remaining shoots to a prominent eye or axil bud. Choose an eye that is facing outwards or towards an open space in the bush, about midway down the stem.

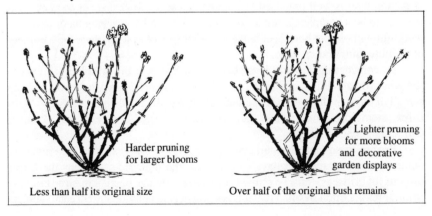

Harder pruning for larger blooms

Lighter pruning for more blooms and decorative garden displays

Less than half its original size

Over half of the original bush remains

Pruning Climbers

Climbers appear to present a formidable job for a novice but, with a little understanding of their habits and by taking the step-by-step approach set out below, their successful pruning should be possible.

Climbers have two different phases of growth. Firstly, the long plain climbing canes start from near the ground, or sometimes on the bend of an earlier cane. They usually grow in autumn and, if left untrained, sprawl up and outwards all over the place. When they are trained into a horizontal or near-horizontal position, the eyes all along the cane burst into short, flowering spurs, always in spring but often also in autumn. This means that on a mature climber there is usually a mixture of new climbing canes and old flowering branches.

Step 1. Cut out all of the dead and sickly wood.

Step 2. Carefully bend the new canes into places where they can fill gaps or where an older, run-down branch needs to be removed. Do not bring the canes below the horizontal as most varieties will not grow "downhill", and do not bend them too sharply as they are often brittle. Tie the canes only lightly at this stage.

Step 3. Cast your eye over the climber and look for strong new canes that will replace old ones (3 or 4 years old). Cut out the old ones and tie down the new ones.

Step 4. The older canes that remain will have many flowering spurs along their length. Cut each of these spurs to half-length, generally leaving 3 or 4 eyes.

Step 5. When the canes, either new or old, have tapered down at the end to a weak point, usually about the last quarter of their length, cut this off.

Step 6. Finally, arrange all the canes into an even lattice of growth over the trellis and tie them into place with soft twine, stockings or other soft ties.

Different varieties of climbers have different levels of natural vigour, and pruning cannot completely override this. If a plant appears too vigorous, you can either allow it to run wider along the trellis or add extra wires to the trellis, allowing the plant to grow higher. If you try to keep it down to a certain size merely by cutting it continually, it will rebound with more young canes, to the point where you are fighting a jungle of canes with no flowers. When the plant has been allowed to reach its natural size it will have exhausted its vigour, and will settle down and flower more freely.

Where to Cut

Roses make their best regrowth from either of two points.

The middle one-third of any stem bears the best eyes. Nearer to the top, the eyes bear weak little flowering heads, while at the bottom the eyes are dormant. The largest leaves on the stem have the best eyes beneath them.

The other point of regrowth is where a stem branches from a lower stem. At the junction there is a ring of tiny folds or dark lines which are potential eyes. Usually, a pair of very vigorous shoots will come from either side of the junction if

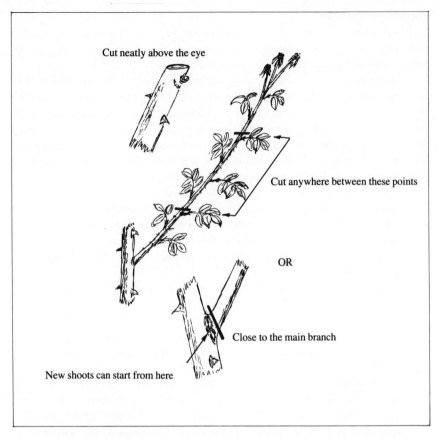

Cut neatly above the eye

Cut anywhere between these points

OR

Close to the main branch

New shoots can start from here

you cut the stem fairly flush with the lower branch. Do not cut so closely that you damage the little base folds.

Much score has been made of the need to cut in a certain way above each eye. It simply amounts to neatness. Cut slightly above the bud, about the diameter of the stem, and sloping slightly away. If you cut too close to the eye, the resultant stem may break off in the wind, and if you leave too much it looks untidy and does not heal over cleanly.

Watershoots and Suckers

These are terms that are sometimes misunderstood by new rose growers. They are sometimes used as if they are synonymous, and the pruning treatments are also misunderstood. The treatment of both is very important, so it is essential to know which is which and treat them accordingly.

Think of the sucker as a parasite to the rose, something to be got rid of, something that will otherwise overrun the plant. The sucker is a growth from the rootstock which has started because of root damage, severe pruning, a diseased plant or poor nursery practice. The root system is usually more vigorous than the variety that is budded to it, and thus it is constantly trying to start new shoots from even the most latent eyes. When the plant comes under stress for reasons that I have mentioned, the rootstock literally bursts out and forms a strong, but totally unwelcome, cane.

Suckers can be first recognized as foreign-looking branches growing amongst the plant. They have a long, climbing habit and seldom flower, certainly never in the autumn. A further check will show that the growth is coming from clearly below the bud-union, even as far as 100–200 mm from the plant. Remove these as soon as possible. In order to make the most thorough removal of the sucker, wait until the soil is damp and the cane is mature enough to pull, then wrench it from the bush. By doing this you will remove most of the base eyes and thus discourage regrowth, but to be doubly sure, expose the area from where it was severed and pare away the side of the junction. Do not merely cut off the sucker at ground level, as your single cane will soon become eight or ten! If you do not keep suckers in check they will soon overrun the legitimate bush.

Watershoots, on the other hand, are very strong legitimate shoots that usually start from the crown of the bush and in one flush of growth soar to the top of the bush. Their name comes from their soft, sappy appearance in the initial growth. Watershoots make up the new framework of the bush and therefore must be nurtured. Keep them staked if the wind is likely to break them when young, and allow them to fully mature before cutting them in any way. When pruning, do not cut heavily into the main stem but merely remove the flower-heads, or about half of the branchlets on a multiple-headed watershoot.

Hygiene

I have already mentioned the need to sterilize your pruning tools, especially your secateurs, between use on each plant, with a disinfectant such as sodium hypo-cholorite (household bleach). This will prevent the spread of certain diseases.

When you have finished the actual pruning, trim off all the old leaves, pick up the prunings and any other fallen leaves and burn them. This will destroy a good number of fungal spores and insect eggs that may be overwintering on the plant. It should not be necessary to seal large cuts with a pruning mastic, provided that the pruning cuts are neat and flush.

Finally, before any new soft shoots appear, spray the plant and the ground beneath with copper oxy-chloride or Bordeaux mixture at winter strength. This is a preventive spray which should minimize the onset of fungal disease in spring.

Summer Pruning

No doubt you have heard this term and have wondered what it involved. I do not consider summer pruning to be a single operation; rather, it is the practice of removing spent blooms throughout the flowering season. Cutting flowers for use indoors is a form of summer pruning, for you must endeavour to leave some full-sized leaves on the stem from which you cut, and when you are merely removing the dead heads you will cut off one or two of the topmost leaves as well.

CHAPTER SIX

The rose calendar

A month by month guide to what you should be doing, and what to expect from your rose garden throughout the year.

January

Some blooms of mediocre quality. Keep the spent blooms trimmed off, but do not cut blooms with long stems. In hot, dry climates, the branches may become sunburned if allowed to dry and drop their leaves. Therefore, see that the mulch is still intact, and water deeply once a week or more in sandy soils, less in heavy soils. If you are going on holidays, your roses should be safe for a couple of weeks, but in the event of a longer absence, ask a friend to do the watering for you.

Watch for spider mites which produce the appearance of unwatered plants.

February

Give your roses help towards their autumn display by trimming them lightly all over and adding a small handful of rose manure or an N.P.K. mixture. Give them a heavy watering. Continue to water every one or two weeks, depending on the weather.

March

Bushes should be in lush growth, culminating in good-quality blooms by the end of the month. Winter-flowering varieties such as 'Lorraine Lee' and 'Nancy Hayward' should be pruned now.

Pockets of aphids may appear. Wash them off with a jet of water (to give the predators time to catch up) or spray if they get out of hand.

Nursery catalogues are sent out this month; send away for yours from your usual supplier.

April

You should be enjoying your best autumn display of blooms.

Use this period to plan for the future. Decide whether any plants are "passengers", and whether you want to extend your plantings. Visit display gardens, nurseries and rose shows. Order new plants while supplies are good.

Dig out old plants and prepare new areas for winter planting.

Mildew may appear once the nights become cool and dewy.

May

Some good blooms will continue into this month, so keep up with your dead-heading (removing spent blooms) and keep mildew and black spot under control. Prevention now is far easier than cure next spring.

Later in the month you can dig out and shift any plants that need to be moved. If you intend trying your hand at nursery plants, put in the rootstock cuttings now.

June

Only occasional blooms as the plants go dormant.

Plant new plants from now through to August. General nurseries and chain stores receive their supplies this month.

Pruning can commence late this month in mild climates. Plant cuttings of your favourite varieties, using offcuts from pruning if you wish.

July

A busy month for rose growers. (Thank goodness the weather is cool and conducive to working!)

Pruning time in most districts. Collect all prunings and leaves, and burn or compost them. Hoe, rake and tidy up the beds. Spray thoroughly with copper oxy-chloride and then winter oil (tar distillate). Fertilize each rose plant with a handful of rose manure.

August

Pruning and subsequent clean-up time in frost-prone districts.

Finish planting "bare root" nursery plants by the end of the month. Container plants are just coming into their new season.

Sit back and watch them grow.

September

As the ground dries out it is a good time to apply mulch in order to smother the weeds and to conserve moisture.

Bushes should be in strong, spring growth. Support any especially strong soft canes against breakage. Aphids can be damaging, especially to the smallest tips, so keep them in check. Mildew may appear later in the month. "Wilt and dieback" disease is most evident this month, so check any suspicious growth.

October

The main flush of spring blooms will commence late this month or early next month, and the major rose shows are timed to coincide with the peak of the Large-flowered class. Old-world and species roses spread over a longer period with some species commencing in late September, and 'Old European' classes peaking in November.

November

Good-quality blooms continue, especially in the cooler areas and amongst the Cluster-flowered types and the old-world roses.

Trim off the spent blooms as soon as flowering has finished. Spring-flowering varieties, such as species roses and some old-world roses, should be lightly pruned and shaped after flowering.

Bud your nursery plants now, as budding wood becomes mature.

December

Continue regular watering, depending on the weather and soil type. Add a small handful of rose manure, especially if you want a continuing garden display throughout the summer.

Watch out for spider mites during hot, dry spells.

The calendar relates to a temperate climate in the southern hemisphere. In cooler areas, such as southern New Zealand, Tasmania and highland Australia, spring effects could be up to a month later and autumn effects a month earlier. In warmer areas the spring effects are earlier and the autumn pattern occurs later.

CHAPTER SEVEN

What's in a name?

Miniatures, Grandifloras, bush, climbing, ramblers, pillar, shrub, stem and weeping roses

Rose Types and Classifications

Before we get too far into a discussion about roses (especially the more unusual and special purpose roses), it is essential that we understand what is meant by particular terms. Over recent years many different terms and classes have crept into the rose grower's vocabulary, and others have taken on new meanings. This comes home very forcibly when I handle mail orders for roses and try to be sure that what the customer has written is, in fact, what he or she really wants. Some explanations in a moment will illustrate this point.

We must also realize that rose classifications, such as "Large Flowered", "Cluster Flowered", "Miniatures" and "Climbers", do not represent varieties that fit neatly into each classification like peas in a pod. Classifications are a man-made system, developed with a view to grouping certain roses (or any other plants for that matter) into logical groups for the sake of easy reference and identification. This works well most of the time, and it is only when varieties get close to the borderline between one class and another that misunderstanding arises. The breeder of the plant decides what class it should belong to, usually in the light of the parentage of that plant. It is possible, for reasons of public preference or market pressures, for the breeder to classify his/her new introduction on the side of the borderline opposite to that which might be commonly expected.

The accompanying diagram is an effort to show the latest system of rose classification, adopted in 1976 by the World Federation of Rose Societies. In the right-hand column is a list of the classes into which every rose should be able to be allocated.

First, there is the **Large Flowered** class, which is the newer and more descriptive term for the Hybrid Tea (H.T.) class which dominated the rose world for over one hundred years. Most people think of this class of roses when they

What's in a name?

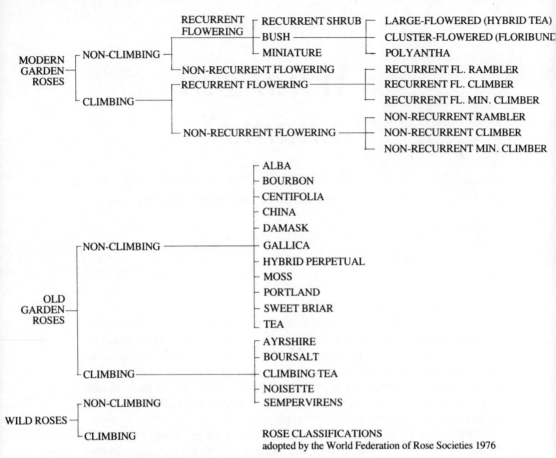

ROSE CLASSIFICATIONS
adopted by the World Federation of Rose Societies 1976

imagine a large, solitary specimen bloom. It is the most widely grown class in Australia and New Zealand.

Cluster Flowered is the term to describe what were previously known as the Floribunda and Floribunda-H.T.-type classes. The early Floribundas were bred in the 1950's and quickly became popular. More recently, they became so interbred with the Large Flowered roses that precise grouping became very difficult. The new Cluster Flowered class embraces varieties with quite large, formal-shaped blooms of multiple or cluster heads, grading down in size to about half-sized blooms.

Polyantha is an old term from late last century, but a few examples ('The Fairy', 'China Doll' and 'Green Ice') are still well known. The flowers are quite small, but they appear in large clusters and, although many are small growers, a few such as 'Orange Triumph' can be quite vigorous.

Patio Roses is a term that I expect you will hear in the not too distant future. There is a trend to grow more and more plants in containers for use both within the house and close by. The increasing number of people living in units and small properties has encouraged this and, not surprisingly, some rose breeders have risen to the occasion. A small range of new roses, between the polyantha and miniature classes, with hardy constitutions and long-lasting blooms, is being released onto the market with a view to filling the needs of the smaller-home owner. These will be marketed as Patio Roses.

Miniatures, as the name quite accurately implies, are small roses in every way. Their blooms, foliage, stems and prickles are all scaled down replicas of their full-sized counterparts. In some ways they resemble Polyanthas, but their foliage and stems are distinctly more demure. 'Fairy Roses' is an alternative, rather quaint, name that is occasionally used for miniature roses.

Grandifloras is the term which was born in 1954 when the well-known 'Queen Elizabeth' came onto the market. It has medium-sized blooms on a vigorous bush, and the enterprising Americans considered that this justified a new classification. Similar varieties have been added to the class over the years but, for all that, the term has never caught on outside the U.S.A.

Bush and **Climber** are quite explicit terms. Most popular roses are of bush (or non-climbing according to the recommendations of the W.F.R.S.) growing habit, which means that they produce branches of modest length, each terminating with a solitary flower or a cluster of blooms, depending on the class. As each branch matures, more lateral branches sprout from lower down, in turn producing more blooms. The overall effect is that of a globular, thickety or vase-shaped bush.

Large Flowered and Cluster Flowered bushes generally range in height from 1 m to over 2 m, and spread the equivalent of about two thirds of their height. Bush miniatures range from 300 mm in height.

A climbing habit means that the rose plant produces long, unflowering canes that are usually quite thin and flexible, often arching to the ground if unsupported. Once these canes have matured, especially when they have been tied into an approximately horizontal position, they produce short, flowering stems which festoon the canes with blossom. Climbers tend to produce most of their canes in autumn and come into flower in the following spring, although the better-performing varieties grow and flower throughout the seasons. In vigour, climbers vary considerably. Some strong-growing varieties measure 6–8 m across and 2–3 m high, but they are more usually 3–5 m across, while miniature climbers will cover 2–3 m. All require additional support in order to keep them in shape.

Climber and **Rambler** are terms that are often used indiscriminately for the same plant. I have not found clear definitions, but I will venture my thoughts.

Climber suggests a stout growing plant whose canes naturally grow upward and must be pulled or trained into a horizontal position. Most of them will not grow below a horizontal or downhill position. Often they are "sports" of bush roses. Ramblers, on the other hand, produce thin, flexible canes that may be draped into almost any position — upwards, horizontal or cascading.

Pillar Roses is a term that has returned to popular use in recent years. As implied, pillar roses are suited to training around a pillar, post or column. In fact, they are merely smaller-growing climbers, possibly miniature climbers, or one of

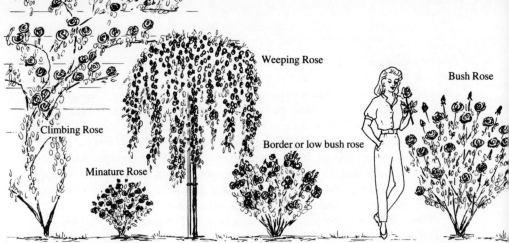

Weeping Rose

Bush Rose

Climbing Rose

Border or low bush rose

Minature Rose

several species or old-world climbers whose natural vigour only takes them to about 2–3 m high.

Shrub roses is a term often used to embrace all of the older and unorthodox roses not covered in the preceding classes. In the strictest sense, all roses are shrubs, but because the early history of roses is scattered with many varied types of roses (not to mention several quite modern roses that cannot logically be placed into any of the existing classes) the term shrub roses is used to take in this diverse, significant and useful collection of nomads.

Species roses, in the broadest sense, means all of the wild roses, many of which have found their way into the gardens (and the hearts) of specialist rose-fanciers.

Hybrid species are a variety which, if not a direct seedling from the original species, carries many of the characteristics of its wild parent.

The Naming of Climbers
Climbing roses occur in two forms.

One, which I will refer to as "natural" climbers, comprises varieties that exist only as climbers. They may be original species such as *R. banksia* and *R. laevigata*, or a climbing class of rose such as the Noisettes, and sometimes they are new roses, specifically bred as climbers. They are named without the prefix "Climbing", e.g. Altissimo, Blackboy, Cocktail, **not** Climbing Altissimo, Climbing Blackboy, or Climbing Cocktail.

The other form of climber occurs when a bush rose "sports" or mutates to a climbing form. Quite unpredictably, a bush rose may produce a long climbing cane. By careful selection and propagation, the new climbing form can be stabilized and established. Such roses are named with the prefix "Climbing", e.g. Climbing Iceberg (often abbreviated to Clg. Iceberg, or Iceberg Clg.).

We have now looked at the most usual and best-known classes of roses. If you develop your rose garden — and your interest — with these classes in mind, you will be well along the way to having a very comprehensive garden.

Stem Roses. A popular variation that is both beautiful and practical, if at times a little misunderstood, are the Stem roses (sometimes known as Standard

50

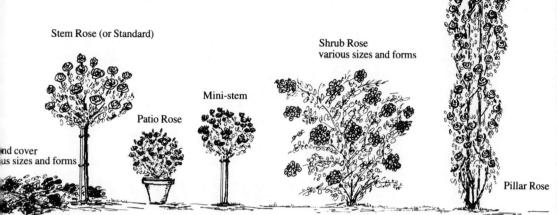

Stem Rose (or Standard)

Shrub Rose
various sizes and forms

Mini-stem

Patio Rose

nd cover
us sizes and forms

Pillar Rose

roses or Tree-roses). These are the roses that grow on the top of a single slender stem. You have probably seen and admired them, even if you have been unsure about how they were created and what sort of roses can be grown on these tall stems. Most rose plants are propagated either as rooted cuttings, or budded onto an understock at ground level. In either case, the rose thickets up from the ground. If the same rose is budded onto a long stem of understock, all of its bushiness will commence at the point of budding (usually about waist high). Any variety of rose, bush, miniature or climber, can be budded onto any length understock, within reason, in order to achieve any of a multitude of effects. Thankfully for the nurserymen, commonsense has prevailed and the selection of Stem or Standard roses has resolved itself into the following three main categories:

Bush roses, which are the most commonly known and grown as stems are budded at a uniform height of 750 mm.

Miniatures, which are budded at a height of 450–500 mm.

The spectacular **Weeping roses**, which are actually cascading ramblers that have been budded at a height of 1200–1800 mm.

Although the usual Stem roses are now a standard 750 mm high, this has not always been the case. When they were enjoying a wave of popularity between the World Wars, they came in four sizes — 2' high was a quarter Standard, 2'6" was a half Standard, 3' was a three quarter Standard, and 4' was a full Standard. As the demand dropped somewhat, three of the sizes were abandoned, leaving only the half Standard. New arrivals from overseas where the other sizes persist are often confused by the terminology but, in Australia, the half standard is now the usual stem rose.

You may also have noticed (and been confused by) the alternative use of the terms ''Stem roses'' and ''Standard roses''. In past years, Australian usage has favoured ''Standard'', the word referring to an upright support, as in standard lamp; or tree or shrub that stands alone without support. However, my experience has shown that many people, usually new gardeners, use the term when referring to the normal bush roses, thinking of ''standard'', or ''the usual''.

In the interests of eliminating confusion, I much prefer the term ''Stem rose'' which is in line with usage in parts of Europe, and I will continue to use the term.

51

CHAPTER EIGHT

What roses can do for your garden

Recommendations — cutting, bedding, general purpose

Large Flowered Roses and Cluster Flowered Roses

I will consider these two classes together, for they have far more common characteristics and uses than they have differences. They represent the majority of all rose plants and are consequently the best-known groups. In addition, modern breeding, especially across the boundaries that existed between the two classes, has so merged the two classes that it is no longer possible to categorically describe some varieties as "Large Flowered" or "Cluster Flowered". I am pleased to see the term "Floribunda" being phased out, for many people have a preconceived bias against the class, based on their limited knowledge of the early, small-flowered clusters. Now that the cluster-flowered types have blooms almost as large, and just as shapely, as the large-flowered types, the grounds for their dislike have disappeared, but their bias continues. I have known many people to voluntarily choose varieties in our display gardens, but when told that they are a lovely selection of floribundas, to suddenly change their minds. Nor is it unknown for rose breeders to classify "borderline" varieties as Hybrid Teas or Floribundas, depending on the preferences of the particular country into which they are being introduced. For instance, in Australia the majority of plants sold are the larger-flowered, while in Europe, especially in Germany, the cluster flowers are distinctly in the lead.

What do the two classes have in common?

Their general habit of growth, the manner in which they carry their blooms, the shape of their blooms and, most importantly, their uses in the home and in the landscape are similar.

In habit of growth, they typically range in height from 1 m to over 2 m and in spread from under 1 m to 1.5 m.

All modern bush roses flower repeatedly throughout the season, in flushes

(Top)   MAGIC CARROUSEL Unusual yet attractive, the growth is really too vigorous to be considered as a true miniature.

(Right)   BABY DARLING A relatively old variety (1964) which still maintains its popularity.

(Bottom left)   STAR TRAIL One of several varieties which 'suntan' from yellow to orange and red in the bright sunlight.

((Bottom right)   STARINA A miniature whose formation is as perfect as any larger variety, and consequently a firm favourite.

(Top left)   STAR TRAIL budded onto a mini-stem 450 mm (18″) tall — a lovely effect and ideal for adding height and interest to the garden.

(Top right)   CLIMBING ICEBERG An ideal tripod specimen.

(Bottom left)   CHINA DOLL A low border rose which literally covers itself with blooms throughout the season.

(Bottom right)   CLG. PINKIE A moderate climber with many potential uses, here trained around a 'permapine' post. Author's garden.

several weeks long and about 6–8 weeks apart.

The flowering season usually begins between late October and mid-November, and extends until pruning time in winter.

Most roses in the two groups bear blooms of the modern traditional form, with a pointed bud opening to a circular outline and high, spiralling centre. However, there are a goodly number of more informal types with a lighter, more airy arrangement of petals, while others feature tight rings of petals in a rosette formation or cupped formation. Just to add a little confusion to the discussion, most roses of either group will form a multiple head (or cluster) on top of a strong watershoot in spring, and even the Cluster Flowered types will throw a good number of single stems on an older, lightly pruned plant.

So you can see why the two groups have more in common than is generally appreciated.

Each variety of rose has its own characteristics apart from the obvious differences between the blooms. Some have glossy leaves, others matt; some carry a thick canopy of foliage, some are sparse; some are tall, some are short, and so on. It is these differences that make up the total desirability of a rose for a certain purpose.

For instance, a variety that consistently grows single shapely blooms on long stems would be ideal for floral arrangements or for cutting blooms for sale. 'Mister Lincoln' (red), 'Eiffel Tower' (pink), 'Mabella' (yellow) and 'Pascali' (white) are good examples.

Varieties that produce consistently large blooms of good form but not necessarily on long stems are used as specimen blooms for competition (or exhibiting as it is called), and are consequently referred to as "exhibition" type roses. 'Red Devil' (light red), 'Peter Frankenfeld' (pink), 'Peace' (yellow) and 'Amatsu-Otome' (yellow) are just a few.

Some varieties have a happy combination of factors that make them ideal just to look at in the garden. A plentiful display of eye-catching blooms carried neatly on a thick, well-rounded plant just asks to be used for this purpose, and the following varieties spring to mind: 'Fidelio' (red), 'Apricot Nectar' (apricot), 'Bettina' (orange) and 'Portrait' (pink). Then there are varieties which combine a fair degree of all of these attributes, and can thus be considered as general-purpose roses. 'Diamond Jubilee' (apricot-yellow), 'Susan Hampshire' (pink) and 'Chrysler Imperial' (crimson) are good examples.

Over the years I have seen many good new roses sink into oblivion without fair trial because their blooms did not possess the traditional form or shape to make an attractive photograph to grace the glossy pages of a nursery catalogue or magazine. Their virtue was in their sheer ruggedness and dependability or in their attractiveness as a garden display; but these are factors that cannot be easily communicated to the new rose buyer — they become apparent only after several years of experience and observation. I feel so keenly about these various aspects that in our annual catalogue I include a feature which draws attention to varieties which are especially suited to cutting, and to certain others more suited to bedding purposes. Those that are not marked for one or other can then be assumed to possess some of both features. In this way I feel sure that we have been able to help people realize that roses are not "just a pretty flower".

It has been truly said that there are no bad roses, but that only some are in fashion at one time. I would modify that slightly and say that there are no bad roses, it all depends for what purpose you want to use them.

The following lists are not long, for I think it is important to mention only those varieties which are really ideal. An extensive, possibly bewildering, selection may not always be obtainable or may be less than suitable for your purposes.

Cutting Roses

Those generally having classically shaped blooms borne singly on good-length stems and having good keeping qualities when cut.

Adolf Horstmann. Soft gold, tinged with copper; the large, gently ruffled blooms keep well (for that colour).

Alexander. Brilliant orange-scarlet; with long, straight stems. Excellent in cool climates, but unsuited in warm areas.

Ambassador. Striking combination of apricot, opening to orange, shaded with gold; on a tall, upright bush.

Blue Moon. Clear cool lilac-blue; with large fragrant blooms and few thorns.

Carina. Medium-large blooms of clear rhodamine pink; particularly consistent and long-lasting.

Carla. A popular and attractive shade of soft salmon; with large double blooms and long stems; fragrant.

Christian Dior. An old favourite; light-red with consistently well-formed blooms; rather prone to powdery mildew.

Double Delight. A spectacular effect and popular choice, with cream blooms richly suffused to the edges with strawberry.

Dr. A. J. Verhage. Smoky yellow blooms that last well (for that colour).

Eiffel Tower. Blooms of clear pink; with especially long buds and long thornless stems; very fragrant.

Esmeralda. Clear rose pink shading distinctly lighter on the reverse; large and well formed.

First Love. Distinctive long, reflexing buds of soft shell pink, shading deeper to the centre.

Galia. Bright coral red, slightly silver on the reverse; borne on long stems.

Hidalgo. Consistent performer in the popular clear red range; plenty of flowers on useful length stems.

Ilona. Medium sized, neat and long-lasting blooms of brick red.

Interview. (known overseas as Interflora). Large, tough-textured blooms of orange-scarlet.

John F. Kennedy. Creamy white blooms, sometimes slightly tinged green in the bud.

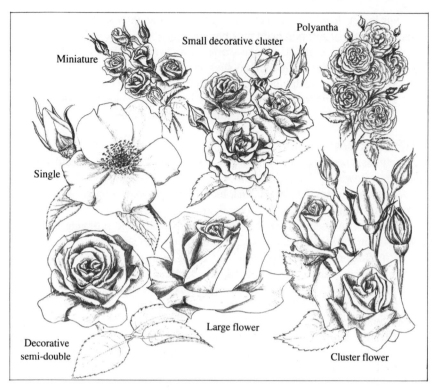

Miniature

Small decorative cluster

Polyantha

Single

Decorative
semi-double

Large flower

Cluster flower

Lady X. Daintily reflexing buds of pastel lilac; long thornless stems.

Mabella. Plenty of moderately large, eye-catching blooms of mimosa yellow.

Marjorie Atherton. Large soft yellow on stout stems; featured on the Australian 27-cent postage stamp in May 1982.

Mercedes. Crisp double blooms of medium size; Granada red, but may fade in hot, dry weather.

Mister Lincoln. Rich dusky red; very fragrant and with long stems.

Papa Meilland. Deeper red than Mister Lincoln; large, beautifully formed, fragrant blooms.

Pascali. Magnolia white, with elegantly formed reflexing blooms and clean, soft green foliage.

Patricia. Salmon pink blooms of medium size; borne very freely.

Peter Frankenfeld. Consistently well-formed blooms of deep rose pink; on useful-length stems.

Prominent. Exquisitely well-formed blooms of bright orange; of medium size; rather prickly.

Romantica. Crisp blooms of rich coral-orange; on very long, clean stems.

Royal Highness. Very pale shell pink; the blooms are large and elegant; borne on long stems with few thorns.

57

Sonia. A leading commercial cut flower, but grows well in the open; constant supply of soft porcelain pink blooms.

Super Star. Brilliant orange-scarlet; was very popular but is being hard pressed by more recent introductions such as Galia.

Sylvia. Clear, fresh pink; on a tall bush.

Thais. Buff-yellow-veined and shaded bronze; large blooms on stout stems.

Virgo. An old favourite which produces plenty of elegant, pure white buds.

Bedding Roses

The emphasis here is on a tidy habit of growth, a thick covering of healthy foliage and a free-flowering display of blossom.

Apricot Nectar. A large, thick bush with light matt foliage and a constant showing of light apricot blooms; very fragrant.

Bettina. A medium sized spreading bush with large reflexing blooms of golden-orange which deepen to copper-orange in warm weather.

Charleston. One of the showiest "changing colour" roses, especially for warmer climates; the yellow buds quickly turn deep red in the sun; fairly low-growing; it is wonderful in a row rather than mixed with others.

Chorus. One of the most dazzling signal reds of all; with clusters of medium blooms on a moderate bush.

Circus. One of the older cluster roses, but still unbeaten in shades of sunset yellow and sunset orange, to coral-pink; lowish bush.

Dearest. Clusters of medium sized rosette blooms of delicate salmon pink; a moderate-height bush; very fragrant.

Duet. Not always instantly appealing, but will win you over with its sheer consistency and effect; a tall bush covered with deep pink blooms shading paler to the centre.

Elizabeth of Glamis. Fragrant and nicely formed blooms of unfading rich salmon; on a bushy bronze-tipped plant of over-average height.

Granada. Dainty buds and very fragrant blooms of light red shading yellow, which flower very early; on a moderately large bush.

Iceberg. (known in Europe as 'Schneewitchen'). Surely the greatest bedding rose of our times. Small sprays of dainty white blooms are borne constantly on a tall bush of glossy bright green foliage. A variety that goes well with anything, or as a specimen on its own.

Kalinka. A thick, spreading bush featuring bronze growing-tips; virtually thornless; bearing informal blooms of dainty porcelain pink.

Lilac Charm. Simple five-petalled pastel lilac blooms in large clusters on a low bush.

News. Strikingly different; with large informal blooms of rich mauve scattered over a medium-sized bush.

Pink Parfait. An earlier Floribunda which deserves to be better-known; beautifully formed medium-sized blooms of carmine shading to soft orange; on a dense light green bush.

Portrait. Quite large well-formed blooms of deep pink shading lighter to the centre; the bush is fairly tall and upright and carries the blooms nestled against the foliage.

Queen Elizabeth. One of the best-known roses of all; perfect for tall hedges and backgrounds; decorative clear pink blooms borne singly but freely on a hardy plant.

Rusticana. This could aptly be described as an orange-scarlet form and an ideal companion for the famous 'Iceberg'; size, growth and habit of flowering are similar, while the foliage is deeper and bronze tipped.

Scherzo. Eye-catching blooms of scarlet with a distinct silvery white reverse; large clusters on a lower than average-height bush.

Susan Hampshire. Remarkably free-flowering for such large double blooms; the colour is deep clear pink; very fragrant and borne on a thick matt green, medium-height bush.

Sweet Home. Camellia-like deep pink blooms of medium size borne singly but freely.

Tequila. A lovely combination of bronzy foliage against the orange-scarlet blooms shading gold to the centre; quick to repeat on a tall willowy bush.

General-purpose Roses

As the name implies, these varieties have a fair degree of both cutting and bedding qualities. They are therefore a safe choice if you are in any doubt about your requirements.

Amatsu-Otome. Large soft yellow blooms (not unlike 'Peace' without the pink edge) on a medium-height bush of thick soft green foliage.

Baronne E. de Rothschild. The distinctly "old world" ruby red blooms with a silver reverse are strongly scented; large blooms, sometimes in clusters, on a tall glossy bush.

Camelot. Could be likened to a coral-red 'Queen Elizabeth'; has large decorative flowers, strong growth and a hardy constitution.

Charles de Gaulle. The lilac-blue blooms are large, double and fragrant, and have a warmer tone than earlier blues; the bush is thick and compact.

Chrysler Imperial. Large nicely formed blooms of dusky red; very fragrant; borne on a lowish, compact matt-green bush.

Diamond Jubilee. Distinctly in the "old world" tones of soft buff-apricot, the blooms are of good size and form, carried on a disease-resistant bush of moderate, compact habit; very fragrant.

Fidelio. A sustained display of medium-sized orange-scarlet blooms which deepen attractively in the sunlight, and last well both on and off the bush; the bush is tallish and well rounded; fragrant.

Fragrant Cloud. Arguably the most fragrant modern rose, the blooms are a lovely brilliant orange-scarlet; large and well formed; on a bush of moderate-height.

Friesia. Crisp, attractively rippled blooms of intense yellow; very fragrant;

59

borne in small clusters on an average-height bush.

Gold Bunny. A wonderful new introduction. Each of the medium-sized clear yellow blooms is of classic form; it is seldom without flowers; the soft green foliage of the medium-sized bush is thick and virtually immune to disease.

Just Joey. Instantly appealing blooms with softly rippling petals; the large fragrant blooms are coppery-orange; on a moderate, spreading bush.

Kabuki. Warm yellow blooms which open to a softer, ruffled effect; on a glossy bush of moderate size; fragrant.

Manou Meilland. Hard to beat for the number of blooms produced, coupled with the all-round hardiness of the glossy foliage; the medium-sized blooms are beautifully formed and deep pink; the bush is of moderate size.

Michele Meilland. A distinctly feminine rose with elegantly formed blooms that vary between soft peach and apricot tones; clean matt foliage and moderate growth; very fragrant.

Montezuma. An unspectacular rose that wins friends with its hardy reliability; good-sized blooms of orange-pink on a tall bush.

Oklahoma. One of the deepest red roses; large and fragrant but inclined to be globular; nevertheless bears plenty of blooms.

Peace. The best-known and most widely grown rose of all time; after 40 years still one of the best; large soft yellow blooms edged pink; on a thick stocky bush of medium size.

Polynesian Sunset. Clusters of good-sized and very dainty blooms of coral-orange; grows to above average height.

Princess Margaret. A clear mid-pink rose which continues to perform well through all weathers and all seasons; large fragrant blooms on a tall upright bush.

Red Devil. Varying between deep pink and light red, with a slightly lighter reverse; the blooms are as big and stout as the bush that bears them; fragrant.

Samourai. Deep glowing red rosette blooms in clusters; resistant to heat and cold; bush is fairly tall and quite hardy.

Tamango. Rose red blooms deepening to garnet red upon opening; hardy in all weathers, besides lasting well when cut; foliage is also extremely disease-resistant — in short, a minimum-care rose.

Violet Carson. Subtle shades of peach softly blending to biscuit and gold on the reverse and base of the petals; moderate clusters on a bronze-tipped bush.

Low Bordering Roses

Especially suited to use as plantings of one variety or alternate contrasting colours. Heights range from 500 mm to 1 m.

Charleston. Described in the Bedding selections; especially suited to planting as a one-variety border.

China Doll. One of the lowest borderers; it bears huge heads of rich china pink blooms almost to the ground.

Dreamland. Semi-single soft pink blooms of medium size.

Edelweiss. A soft cream form similar to 'Dreamland'; both varieties display their blooms continuously on low, compact bushes.

Europeana. Clusters of compact, rich crimson blooms complemented by rich green foliage which features maroon growing-tips; a most pleasing effect and a good companion for either 'Dreamland' or 'Edelweiss'.

Green Ice. The small double blooms are white, distinctly tinged green, especially in the cooler weather; foliage is thick and attractively glossy, and arches out to form virtually a ground cover; up to 0.5 m high.

Lilac Charm. Delightfully simple lilac blooms with gold stamens; borne in large clusters.

Marlena. Exceptionally free-flowering; with small clusters of informal rich crimson blooms; usually 600 mm high.

Petite Folie. Virtually a stronger growing miniature, up to almost 1 m; the small coral-orange blooms last well both on the bush and when cut, while the habit is attractively compact.

The Fairy. Especially useful for ground covering effects, even spilling over embankments. Sprays of tiny china pink blooms throughout the season.

Glasshouse Roses

Over the past few years you could not have failed to notice more and more beautifully cultured roses appearing in florist shops. The great majority of these have been grown in glasshouses or, more correctly, controlled environment houses, where they are produced without blemish or disease, and remarkably consistent in shape and size. There is a strong temptation to want to grow varieties just like them. Alas, you will be disappointed, for even if you are able to buy those particular varieties (and most are not stocked by general nurseries) the results will be far different when grown out of doors in the average garden. Glasshouse roses have been bred for a specific purpose and they are perfect only when their special growing requirements are met. To grow them in your garden would be like using a racehorse for drawing a plough.

It would be far more satisfactory to be guided by the special recommendations in this book.

Growing Roses in Containers

The current popularity of small inner suburban homes and gardens, and of informal gardens, has seen a marked trend towards growing more and more plants in containers. Roses have been included in this, and many people are now asking whether they can be grown in pots, and about suitable pots and soil mixtures.

The short answer is that roses grow quite well in containers, provided that you give them regular and sensible attention. You cannot neglect them, for they do require more attention than more traditional pot-plants. When container-grown roses are needed in your plans, or if there is just no other way that you can grow any roses, they are worth the effort.

A container may be a traditional pot, a barrel, a tub, a hollow log, a foundry crucible (rare, but delightful effect), a planter or window-box, an upturned drainage pipe or even an old iron kettle. Anything will do — and here you can let your imagination have its head — provided that it drains well and holds adequate soil.

To look right, i.e. in proportion, the container should be somewhat smaller than the ultimate diameter of the rose bush but, as roses are gross feeders, it should contain as much soil as possible without looking too large.

Ordinary garden soil is not good enough for container growing, but on the other hand I find the inorganic commercial mixes may be too loose. If using a commercial mix, add one-third to one-half of garden loam or rich top-soil.

If mixing your own, use:

1 part loam
1 part peat moss or crushed pine bark
1 part sharp or washed sand
1 dessertspoon Osmocote to 1 (10 litre) bucket of potting mix.

Your container plant will be something of a feature or specimen, so pay particular attention to your choice of variety. All roses will grow equally well in pots but some are neater growing and more compact and will therefore look better.

Miniatures, especially some mini-stems, are ideal. So are some lower Floribundas, while the ground covering varieties and some species look fine in more informal settings.

Planter boxes and window-boxes should be treated like any other containers, using the same potting soil, and watering and fertilizing regime. Large tubs which might otherwise be too large for your requirements can often be planted out with several plants, thus creating a mini-garden of roses. Roses can also be planted in hanging baskets. Spreading varieties like 'The Fairy' and 'Green Ice' ask to be used for this purpose, as do the hanging mini-climbers, 'Red Cascade', 'Orange Cascade', 'Clg. Baby Darling' and 'Snow Carpet'.

Containers should be watered regularly, and the drainage holes checked for free drainage. Every few weeks give the soil an extra-heavy watering to wash out accumulated salts. Should the rose become dry, its leaves will shrivel and fall; however, it is seldom enough to kill the plant. In a couple of weeks, given regular watering, new leaves will appear, although it will be a few more weeks before the rose has fully recovered its former appearance.

For fertilizing, the slow-release Osmocote type, or tablets or spikes are suitable, and you can use folia fertilizers if you want to push the plants on for a special purpose. Be sure that the formula is a complete N.P.K. mixture, not a high-nitrogen formula.

Varieties Suitable for Growing in Containers

Small pots (5–10 litre capacity)

Practically all miniatures, especially:

Cecile Brunner   (pink)
China Doll   (pink)
R. chinensis semperflorens (red)

Green Ice	(greenish white)
Marlena	(red)
Petite Folie	(coral)
The Fairy	(pink)
Most mini-stem roses	

Medium-sized pots (10–20 litre capacity)

Angel Face	(lavender)
Charleston	(yellow to red)
Chorus	(bright red)
Dearest	(pink)
Europeana	(deep red)
Friesia	(yellow)
Gold Bunny	(yellow)
Great News	(purple)
Just Joey	(amber)
Manou Meilland	(deep pink)
Michele Meilland	(pale pink)
Old Master	(red splashed white)
Pink Parfait	(pink tones)
Viridiflora	(green)

Low cascading effects in medium-sized pots

Frau Dagmar Hastrup	(lilac)
Nazomi	.(pale pink)
Orange Cascade	
Red Cascade	
Sea Foam	(white)
Yesterday	(lilac-pink)

Large pots (20–30 litre capacity)

Apricot Nectar	(soft apricot)
Buff Beauty	(buff yellow)
Duet	(pink tones)
Fidelio	(red)
Granada	(autumn tones)
Iceberg	(white)
Nevada	(cream single)
Portrait	(pink)
Queen Elizabeth	(pink)
Rusticana	(orange)
Tamango	(red)
Large-growing stem roses	
Pillar roses	
Rugosa hybrids	
Weeping roses	

Climbers and Ramblers

Climbers are one of the most rewarding classes of roses, and one of the least understood.

They are rewarding because they lend themselves to a host of interesting uses in the garden, limited only by the imagination of the gardener; but misunderstood by people who expect them to do things for which they are not suited, while not using them for purposes for which they are ideal.

I will refer to climbers and ramblers together because ramblers are merely a more flexible and cascading type of climber.

The bush rose that spontaneously sends out climbing canes will have flowers and foliage similar to the bush form, but the long canes are usually without blooms until they have matured and lain horizontally, whereupon the flowering stems burst from them. Generally, these climbers flower best in spring and make their strongest growth in autumn, producing canes ready for the following spring.

However, there is a catch. Just because a bush rose is good, it does not necessarily follow that the climbing version will be equally successful. Often, the climbing canes are so rampant that they scarcely find time to flower, so choose varieties that you know are good performers, or seek the advice of a reliable nursery.

In most cases, the climbers that have been hybridized specifically for the purpose will be more satisfactory. They usually flower over a long period (in fact they often equal the bush rose in this regard), and their habit of growth is often softer, more elegant and more easily trained.

Most of the natural climbers originally came from the species rambler, *R. wichuraiana*, a single white with a delightful apple scent, which grows flat along the ground with canes as limp as rope. Consequently, many of its close relatives have similar cascading habits and can be trained into every conceivable position — upwards, downwards and along anything. Others came from *R. multiflora*, making the growth more stout and self supporting.

To summarize, climbers range from cascading to upright self supporting plants, and their vigour varies from 2 m to a sizeable 10 m across and up to 3 or 4 m high, and all sizes in between. Some have large formal blooms like their bush counterparts, while others have masses of smaller, more casual displays. Some flower throughout the season, while others flower only in spring but with such a display that you would forgive them this "failing". With these resources available, small wonder that there are a multitude of uses and positions for them.

One of the most common uses of climbers is to hide something unsightly, e.g. a corrugated iron fence, a neighbour's shed or a fowl yard. They can be used to camouflage a dead tree that is too hard to dig out or, strategically placed, they can hide a power pylon or distant factory chimney.

Strategically placed, climbers can also screen you from next door's gaze, even from a second-storey window, and climbers planted across the back garden can screen your swimming-pool or barbecue area from unwelcome eyes (you may remember how nearly every country outdoor lavatory had a 'Dorothy Perkins' climbing in front of the door).

Use climbers to soften hard architectural features such as an expanse of wall, foundation build-ups, or carport or verandah posts.

Strong climbers can cover a pergola and create cool summer shade, and conveniently drop their leaves to allow winter sun to come through when it is so welcome.

All these suggestions fulfill practical purposes and give a breathtaking display of colour, and often fragrance, into the bargain.

Obviously, climbers need supports on which to be trained. Sheets of galvanized garden mesh are easy to erect and maintain but, of course, they must be securely supported by stout posts. Tightly strained fencing wires spaced 200 mm apart are good, and I have had my best success with sheep fencing wire tightly strained between posts. This is usually made in sets of five horizontal wires interlocked with vertical wires 300 mm apart. Timber battens are good, but give thought to how you are going to paint them when the time comes. Your climber will need some support when being trained up a pillar or post. Garden mesh rolled into a tube 300–400 mm in diameter and fixed around the post will give you a chance to train the canes around and upwards as it grows, and the mesh is not too conspicuous when bare. A household fence of the usual 1.5 m is too low for most climbing varieties, but by using the existing posts of the fence and extending your wires or battens up a further 600 mm to 1 m, it will comfortably accommodate most. Avoid using chicken wire or chain wire fencing where possible, but if you must use it, resist the temptation to thread the canes through the wire for, as they expand, they can become choked by the wires.

Climbers will thrive in most positions except in shade. When planted on the south side of a fence they will flower mostly on the top where they are in the sunlight. When planted in a cold, draughty area they will not be at their best, but they seem to tolerate this better than their bush counterparts, so it may be worth giving them a trial in such a spot. They will withstand hot western aspects better than bush roses, but bright galvanized iron often reflects too much heat. In any case, do not let them become too dry or defoliated by spider mite because, as they lose their protective covering of leaves, the stems can become sunburned and seriously set back the plant.

You may wish to grow a climber in an area that is otherwise completely covered with paving. I have seen climbers grown quite successfully in tubs or barrels, but remember to maintain regular feeding and watering, for the climber is a big plant and its appetite is proportional. It is better to get the climber into the ground if possible. Lift the paving slabs for an area of half a square metre or cut the concrete with a masonry saw. Be sure to remove any builders' rubble that has inevitably been buried under the paving, and replace it with good top soil.

Recommended Climbers
• Pillar Roses
(Small climbers for use on tripods, poles and pillars; from 2 m to 3 m high.)

Cocktail. Particularly brilliant, with single medium-sized blooms of signal red with a distinct golden eye; flowers almost continually.

Danse de Sylphes. Could be likened to a recurrent-flowering 'Paul's Scarlet'; medium-sized blooms of orange-scarlet in small clusters; growth is thick and freely branching.

Handel. The blooms are an interesting combination of cream with carmine-pink margins which are especially prominent in cool weather; double blooms of moderate size.

Iceberg Clg. A lovely effect with plenty of decorative white blooms against thick glossy green foliage.

Lady Hillingdon Clg. A distinctive older rose with dainty nodding blooms of old gold contrasting with the distinctly bronzy growth; blooms from very early in the spring.

Pinkie Clg. Small button-hole blooms of pink tones, usually in clusters; very thick foliage and — good news — completely thornless.

Scarlet Queen Elizabeth. Often sold as a tall bush rose, this must be considered as an ideal pillar rose, with its free display of large, cup-shaped bright orange blooms.

Pink Perpetue. As the name suggests, the blooms are very recurrent, rose pink and of moderate size with rosette form.

• Screen Climbers
(3–5 m across, free-flowering, with thick foliage.)

Allgold Clg. The thick glossy green canopy of foliage setting off the bright yellow blooms make it ideal as a screen.

Benvenuto. Medium-sized blooms of deep crimson on a medium climber which branches freely to produce a thick screen.

Clair Matin. Dainty, smallish blooms of salmon pink are borne incredibly freely on a soft matt green climber, giving a ''modern old-fashioned'' effect.

Fugue. The medium-sized deep crimson blooms are borne in small clusters, and keep well when picked.

Golden Showers. Another freely branching climber with glossy green foliage and good-sized, decorative golden blooms; few thorns.

Kalinka Clg. An almost thornless climber which is freely covered with medium-sized blooms of porcelain pink; thick soft green foliage.

Meg. The semi-single blooms of crisp salmon-apricot have delightfully contrasting red stamens; spectacular in spring and repeats if the seed hips are removed.

Michele Meilland Clg. Large blooms of a most elegant shape, with subtle tones of soft apricot to salmon.

Rusticana Clg. Recommended for a colourful display, the vermillion-orange blooms of good form and medium size are set against thick glossy foliage; few thorns.

Summer Snow. Featuring a combination of massed, small white blooms and thornless light green foliage; a good decorative effect.

Zepherine Drouhin. This old Bourbon rose bears medium blooms of cerise-red on a bronze-tinged bush which is completely thornless; fragrant.

• Strong Climbers

(Suitable for covering large areas, training over pergolas or rambling through trees. Others are mentioned in the section on old world climbers, page 97.)

Altissimo. Bearing beautiful, large and crisp single blooms of clear rich red; constantly in bloom, making it very popular for such an unorthodox rose.

Bettina Clg. Large orthodox blooms of deep gold to orange; eye-catching and reliable.

Bonica

Dorothy Perkins. Its well-known rose pink clusters and the mutation Excelsa (deep pink) make spectacular masses in spring, with dense cascading habit for the remainder of the year.

Lorraine Lee Clg. Another older variety; especially useful for providing a winter display of very fragrant pink blooms.

Mermaid. Not recommended for the faint-hearted, as it is very vigorous and thorny, but the display of large single yellow blooms throughout the year, and the healthy glossy green foliage, make it worthwhile.

Nancy Hayward. From the same breeding as Lorraine Lee and thus a true winter bloomer; bears large, crisp tomato red single blooms which cut well.

Peace Clg. This large yellow rose edged pink needs no introduction except to say that the climber is every bit as good as the bush form.

Princess Margaret Clg. A well-known orthodox clear pink variety which must be included for its reliability in all weathers, and consistent display.

Samourai Clg. The large rosette-like blooms of glowing crimson are good in all climates, especially hot weather.

Very Special Roses

Many people are fascinated by what is the biggest, the smallest, the most and so on of a subject. Here are a few extremes of the rose world.

Voted "The Best Rose" by successive World Rose Conventions — 'Peace' (1974), 'Queen Elizabeth' (1977), 'Fragrant Cloud' (Duftwolke (1980), 'Iceberg' (1983).

Most popular rose currently — 'Iceberg'.

Most popular rose ever — 'Peace'.

Oldest rose continuously in commerce — 'Cecile Brunner'.

Earliest cultivated rose — 'Quatre Saison' (*R. damascena bifera*).

Largest bloom — 'First Prize'.

Longest bud — 'Eiffel Tower'.

Longest stems — 'Eiffel Tower', 'Romantica'.

Most petals — 'Dame Edith Helen', 'Korde's Perfecta'.

Most fragrant — 'Fragrant Cloud', 'Chrysler Imperial'.

Brightest colours — 'Chorus' (red), 'Alexander' (orange), 'Friesia' (yellow).

Best stripes — 'Harry Wheatcroft' (modern), 'Variegata di Bologna' (old).

Smallest blooms — *R. banksia*, *R. multiflora*, 'Yellow Bantam', 'Perla de Montserrat'.

Smallest bushes — 'Yellow Bantam', 'Marilyn'.

Largest plant — *R. banksia*, *R. gigantea*.

Fastest-growing climber — *R. laevigata*, 'Silver Moon'.

Most impenetrable barrier — 'Mermaid'.

Unusual colours and effects — 'Double Delight', 'Paradise', 'Cafe', 'Vesper', 'Victoriana', 'Great News', 'Imp', 'Old Master', 'Kronenbourg', 'Chinese Green Rose'.

CHAPTER NINE

Landscaping

*Broad concepts, suggested placements,
beds, specimen plants, terraces and patios,
planter boxes, miniatures, public gardens*

It has been claimed that roses are so interesting and adaptable that a whole garden could be landscaped with them, for they provide every necessary size and form. I do not propose to defend that claim, but it serves to illustrate that roses are a most versatile plant. Too often, we think of roses only as the blooms which appear in glossy magazines and catalogues, at rose shows or in floral bouquets, and we lose sight of the fact that, as a spectacle, a rose plant covered with blossoms can be one of the features of the garden. Even if you never cut a bloom to take inside, your roses can easily justify their place in the landscape.

The word ''landscaping'' is very freely used these days. I suppose that, in its simplest sense, it merely means the design and construction of a garden scene. It implies something of the aesthetic, but you should not be frightened off by this for many beautiful gardens have been created with the gardener's preferences and feeling for what looks right. It is not necessary to plan your garden lay-out down to the last pebble, but a broad concept sketch is advisable. Let your thoughts flow freely, and make your plan without too many harsh straight lines and unnecessary details. Think simply and boldly, restrained only by immovable constraints such as the house and boundaries, doorways, gates and driveways. Be prepared to do a lot of your planning in the actual garden, viewing the area from several key locations, to see in your mind's eye how it will look when completed and fully grown. It is even better if you can sketch the imagined scene as viewed from the front gate, from the doorways, through the windows, and from the patio. You may need privacy here or a clear view there; you may need some colour here or some shade there; so use the various plants as though they are colours on an artist's palette, to be put here and there to create your own landscape.

It is not only the appearance of the garden that should concern you; it should also have a feeling of its own — cosy, restful and intimate. Create sheltered sunny areas for winter and cool shady areas fanned by evening breezes for summer. Do not forget the elusive charm of fragrance in the garden, issuing from blossoms and foliage as you brush by. The feeling underfoot is important too — the coolness of a lawn, the spring of deep litter mulch, the utility of a cobblestone path or the clip-clop of a wooden bridge. It is into the resulting scene that we place our roses — the bushes, the climbers, the miniatures and the many other useful and unusual plants.

Let us start by asking what roses can contribute to the garden. First and foremost, they can give colour in many shades and effects, in flowers large and small, pastel and brilliant, and for an extended period which in our temperate climates can be from eight to ten months of the year.

Secondly, they provide a wide range of forms: cute miniatures, typical bushes, strong climbers and spreading ground covers; they can be low compact bushes, or mounted on elegant stems, or cascading weepers. Although some people think of rose bushes as being fairly uniform, some provide unusual but attractive foliage, autumn-tinted foliage, displays of hips (seed pods) or distinctive thorns.

Thirdly, roses ask for very little special attention compared to the return that they give, yet with just a little more effort they can be breathtaking. They will forgive complete neglect, fire, drought and flood (as recent experiences in Australia have proved), and will come back when good conditions return.

The fragrance of roses must surely be their crowning glory, the characteristic which endears them to most people. The soft fragrance of roses undoubtedly puts the final seal of perfection onto any garden.

For all that, roses are not used to best advantage in many private and public gardens. Their use is often unimaginative, a slavish copy of the gardens down the street. Although the use of roses is limited only by your imagination, there are a few ground-rules to smooth the way.

When I plan a garden, I often use blocks or lines of one variety of roses. The traditional row of mixed roses along a front fence would look much better, in my opinion, if it comprised one carefully chosen variety forming a uniform hedge. This creates the illusion of a more expansive row. It is neater because there are no ups and downs caused by the uneven habit of mixed varieties, and all of the roses will flower at the same time. The same can be done with other rose plantings such as beds, dividing screens and borders. Other advantages of multiple plantings of few varieties are that you can cut a goodly number of blooms of one variety for floral arrangements, and it is easier to learn the quirks of each, so culture and maintenance are easier. If you are in doubt, try a small block planting next time and see if you are not convinced by the result. The "botanic garden" effect (i.e. one of everything) can best be used in blocks or free-form beds, and in functional beds that are kept for special purposes such as cut flowers or exhibition blooms.

Roses are available in many colours and effects, and you could therefore easily imagine that blending them would be difficult. Actually, most rose colours blend surprisingly well. Possible exceptions are some of the new orange-scarlet

PETITE FOLIE Taller than most miniatures (700 to 800 mm), it makes a wonderful thick low maintenance hedge.

Miniatures should be grouped at a focal point of the garden, in this case, by the front entrance to the house.

COCKTAIL (left) and CLAIR MATIN Climbers make an everblooming dividing screen.

FUGUE A tall picket fence provides adequate support. A 5 m. wide climber in one year.

COCKTAIL Effectively hiding an unsightly backyard view.

Massed formal beds give an impression of dignity and grandeur. Veale Gardens, Adelaide.

Sweeping informal beds are associated with undulating ground and random tree patterns. 'Sweet Home' in bloom, Hobart Botanic Gardens.

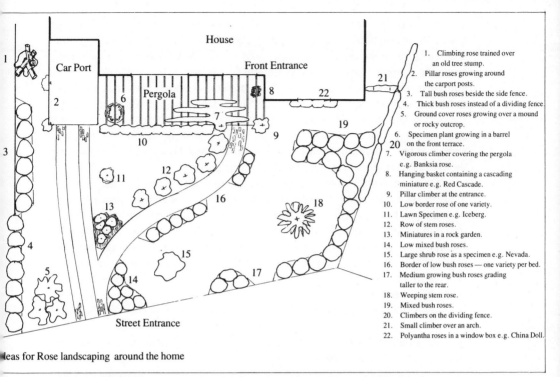

1. Climbing rose trained over an old tree stump.
2. Pillar roses growing around the carport posts.
3. Tall bush roses beside the side fence.
4. Thick bush roses instead of a dividing fence.
5. Ground cover roses growing over a mound or rocky outcrop.
6. Specimen plant growing in a barrel on the front terrace.
7. Vigorous climber covering the pergola e.g. Banksia rose.
8. Hanging basket containing a cascading miniature e.g. Red Cascade.
9. Pillar climber at the entrance.
10. Low border rose of one variety.
11. Lawn Specimen e.g. Iceberg.
12. Row of stem roses.
13. Miniatures in a rock garden.
14. Low mixed bush roses.
15. Large shrub rose as a specimen e.g. Nevada.
16. Border of low bush roses — one variety per bed.
17. Medium growing bush roses grading taller to the rear.
18. Weeping stem rose.
19. Mixed bush roses.
20. Climbers on the dividing fence.
21. Small climber over an arch.
22. Polyantha roses in a window box e.g. China Doll.

Ideas for Rose landscaping around the home

colours, which must be used carefully with rose-pinks to cerise-pinks.

It is more important to grade the sizes of the bushes, especially in single rows where differences in height show up like a saw-tooth silhouette. Get expert advice as to their heights and then plant according to the height criteria rather than the colour blend. You can never be absolutely certain how large a particular rose (or any other plant) is going to grow. Harder or lighter pruning can make some difference but it certainly will not overcome major errors of judgement.

As for the placement or layout of the roses in the garden, by far the most common area used in Australian gardens is along the front fence. This is not a bad arrangement, but be careful in a couple of important respects. Check that street trees are not going to rob the bushes into submission, and grade their heights in some logical way (the lowest near the gate and rising away or the shortest at the highest end of a sloping block, thus giving the illusion of less slope).

Rows are also effective when used as a divider (instead of a fence) between neighbouring house-blocks, or between a driveway and side fence, or beside a garden path. In these cases, I would place the shortest at the front of the block, and graduate backwards to the tallest. For a good hedge effect, plant medium-growing roses about 800 mm apart so that the adjoining bushes lightly intertwine.

Colourful dividing screens can be created by using some of the taller bush roses. These reach up to 1800 mm high, which is taller than the average fence, and are still easy to work around when planted about 1 m apart.

Low borders of roses have been popular for many years. In Victorian times China and Polyantha roses were popular; early this century the Hybrid Polyanthas held sway, then the early Floribundas, and nowadays Miniatures and Patio roses serve the purpose. Lawn edges, pools and fish-ponds, patios, embankments and pathways all ask to be edged by these hardy and showy little bushes. Low, spreading growers, e.g. 'The Fairy' and 'Green Ice', grow up to 400 mm high but 600 mm wide, while 'Charleston', 'Europeana' and 'Edelweiss' reach 1 m high and a similar width. One of the special features of these "littlies" is that they spread to the ground, forming a mass of flowers and foliage that eliminates any thought of having to under-plant with anything else.

Beds and blocks of roses are not used in Australia as much as they deserve. While rows create a sweep or line of colour, beds or roses offer concentrated areas of colour. A bed can be anything from as small as a simple triangle of three plants to the most grandiose park. The effect is always bold and dramatic. Beds may be incorporated into many situations in the domestic garden. Instead of the usual row along the front fence, try little groups of threes or fives placed at intervals — bearing in mind where they will be seen, say between trees, or from the front door or from a window. A little group by the front gate or by the door is always a friendly welcome. Open areas of lawn almost demand to be planted with blocks of roses.

We must not forget the back garden or private garden where roses can be more intimately appreciated, and where a group of roses can convert a difficult corner into a colour spot. Utilitarian beds for cutting and arranging need not look like rows of vegetables. Give the bed a free-form curve, or arch it around a focal point such as a weeping rose, birdbath, sundial or piece of sculpture.

Beds of roses may be in any shape or size, with very few limitations. Generally, a bed should not be so large that you cannot have easy access to all of the plants. As the plan gets bigger, divide it into formal blocks, either with lawn or paved pathways. Free-form beds should look natural, almost as though the surrounding garden pushed the bed into shape. For instance, if there is a hollow curve, let there be a reason for the hollow, such as another tree or shrub within the focus of the curve. Match the style of the rose beds with the style of the rest of the garden. There is no need to be slavish but, generally, an informal free-form garden suggests a rose bed of the same character, while a formal garden of straight lines and circles would accept a similar rose bed.

The accompanying diagrams may give you some ideas.

It is worth mentioning here a few practical points to bear in mind when you are getting down to detailed planning. Some people like to draw out their proposed garden directly onto the ground, and others prefer to work on a scale plan drawn up in comparative comfort at the dining table. Either way works, but for complicated concepts it is far easier to draft your ideas on paper. There is no doubt, however, that in the final stage it is best to mark out the exact placement of each rose plant directly into the garden, before you go off and order or buy your plants.

Roses should be planted at a spacing that will allow them to lightly intertwine

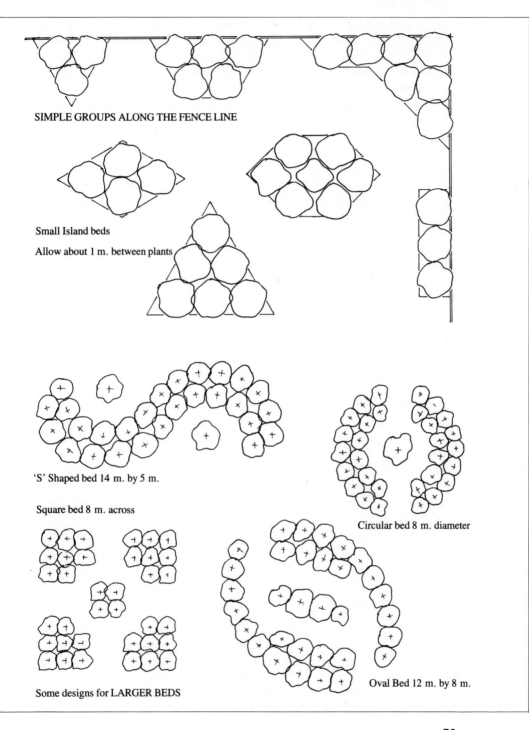

SIMPLE GROUPS ALONG THE FENCE LINE

Small Island beds

Allow about 1 m. between plants

'S' Shaped bed 14 m. by 5 m.

Square bed 8 m. across

Circular bed 8 m. diameter

Some designs for LARGER BEDS

Oval Bed 12 m. by 8 m.

Landscaping

when they are fully grown. Generally, the spacing between plants should be about two thirds of the height that you expect the plants to finally reach, e.g. varieties that reach 1.5 m should be planted about 1 m apart. If you want a dense single row, close up the spacing by another one quarter. If the bed is several rows deep, you must allow extra spacing in the back rows (up to 50% more) for easy access.

Pegging out a large bed may appear to be a daunting task, especially if it is of an unusual shape. By tackling the job in the following steps, you should encounter no problems:

Mark out the total area.

Consider which is the most prominent side (the side from which the bed will be viewed). There may be two prominent sides, or the whole may be equally prominent, but keep this consideration in mind.

Measure a distance of half a rose spacing in from the prominent edge (or edges). Perhaps you have chosen a low variety (one that grows up to 1 m high) for the front row. In that case, you should plant the bushes about 650–700 mm apart; thus the first row will be about 350 mm from the edge.

Working back from the most prominent edge, mark out the second row parallel to the first.

Repeat the procedure until the area has been filled and, as already mentioned, increase the spacing as you get further from the front row.

The most important or prominent row will look neat and even, while the background roses will be widely spaced for easy access, but because of the foreground plants, the gaps at the back will not be noticeable.

People are often concerned about whether to plant their roses in a square pattern or on the diagonal with one plant positioned between each space of the adjoining row. It really does not matter, except that planting in a diamond pattern leaves a triangle of vacant ground at each end of every row. On the other hand, planting on the diamond pattern will sometimes allow you to fit a certain number of rows into a limited space. For instance, two rows usually require about 1.8 m, whereas the diamond pattern requires only 1.2–1.5 m. When planning from a clean start you can make the job quite easy by using a modular grid of 900 mm–1 m, as this is the recommended spacing for average-sized bush roses.

Circular beds always look grand, especially when graded to a high centre. The same rules of layout as for square and diamond-shaped beds apply, and the following list will give you an idea of how many average-sized plants you can fit into various-sized beds:

Diameter of bed	Number of roses
2 m	4
3 m	7 (outer circle) + 1 (centre)
4 m	10 (outer circle) + 3 (centre)
5 m	14 (outer circle) + 6 (centre)
6 m	18 (outer circle) + 10 (second row) +3 (centre)

PLANTING

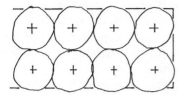

On the square

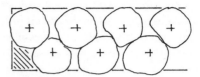

On the diagonal

Creates an awkward waste corner
but enables a narrower bed to be used

Laying out an irregular bed

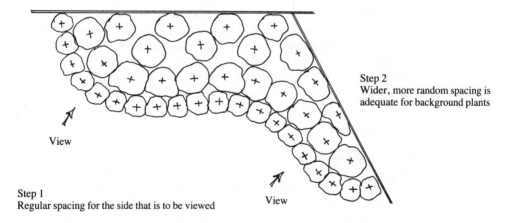

View

Step 1
Regular spacing for the side that is to be viewed

View

Step 2
Wider, more random spacing is
adequate for background plants

Specimen Plants

There are many places in the garden that will be enhanced by the incorporation of
specimen plants in their design. Areas of plain lawn, bare terraces and patios, areas
of low ground-covering shrubbery, and large pots all benefit from the inclusion of
one or more especially selected plants that are neat and attractive in habit, and also
free-flowering.

Many roses are ideal for this purpose. Their natural habit of growth is thick
and well-rounded, they bear their leaves well down to the ground, and produce
blooms that are not only free and colourful but which also nestle back into the
foliage to maintain a well-rounded appearance.

77

Look around your garden to see whether there are any spots that you can use to plant specimen roses. Try out the positions by using a ''dummy'' such as a pot-plant or box. View it from all directions to see whether it looks right; that it does not block a good view but perhaps screens a less than favourable view, and consider whether, when the plant is fully grown, you will be able to pass freely by. It is not necessary to place the specimen in the centre of the space; it may look best off-centre or in the focus of a sweep in the garden. Do not scatter specimen plants around like confetti or the garden will look too busy.

In order to ensure good growth, especially when growing individual plants in lawns that take more than their share of moisture, plenty of clear soil should be left around each rose (ideally a circle of 1 m diameter) or equal to the recommended spacing for that type of rose. Keep the lawn back with a discreet band of steel or timber edging and, if you do not like the thought of bare soil, cover the area with an attractive mulch such as wood or bark chips, pebbles or scoria.

Weeping roses are the most obvious specimen plants, and they are indeed beautiful, but they are by no means the only roses fit for the purpose. The 750 mm stem or standard roses are also very effective, especially if you want to plant the base with low plants such as Sweet Alice, violets and small herbs.

Pillar roses, too, can be featured individually. A climber of only moderate vigour can be trained around a supporting post, forming a column or (as the name implies) pillar of blossom 2.5–3 m high.

Bush roses provide a different effect again, like a ball or vase shape rising from the ground so that companion plants are not necessary.

Varieties that are suitable specimen roses are listed as recommended Bedding Roses on page 58.

Terraces and Patios

Few houses these days would be without a terrace or patio — an extended paved area for sitting out, entertaining and for playing. The direction faced by a terrace or patio largely determines which plants can be successfully grown there.

Roses will grow in an area that receives half a day or more of sunshine, that is not lashed by cold draughts, and is not subjected to the concentrated heat of the afternoon sun. An open, sunny part of a patio is ideal. If you have a patio paved with one of the many types of paving bricks or blocks which are currently available, you can easily lift away a suitable section and plant your roses. Where space permits, a weeping rose looks superb (a large shrub rose achieves a similar effect at less cost), and smaller bushes or stem roses will serve a smaller area very well. Lift out an area of between 600 mm and 1 m square; remove any rubble or rubbish and replace it with good soil before planting. Surprisingly, the rose roots will grow freely beneath the paving, which acts like a mulch for the water that seeps down between the blocks.

If your patio is an expanse of in situ concrete it is possible, with a modern masonry saw, to remove a suitable area. This is especially useful when concrete has been laid solidly from house to fence, and you dearly wish to grow something to brighten the cheerless expanse of cement.

Planter Boxes

Planter boxes may be in various forms and locations in the garden. Several years ago brick boxes were common, beside a wall or protruding from a house. More recently, in a move towards using natural materials, boxes made of sleepers, pine logs and rocks have become popular. All of these arrangements make suitable rose beds, provided that the usual conditions of sunlight, soil and watering are observed. The soil should be prepared as for a pot, with up to half peat moss (or crushed pine bark), and sharp sand if the soil is heavy. Watering is more critical, for the box must be free-draining in order to avoid waterlogging. This means that watering must be more regular, which, in turn, means regular feeding, preferably with slow-release pellets or spikes. If the bottom of the planter box is open to the natural soil beneath, so much the better, for the roots will soon find their way there.

I am often asked, by rather desperate gardeners, how roses can be successfully grown near to robbing trees and shrubs. The following method is worth a try.

Make a planter box of the size and materials of your choice, but see that its top is at least 300 mm above ground. Line the bottom (which should be at ground level) with heavy, black mulching plastic. Cut several drainage holes around the edges of the plastic at points where you can easily watch for invasion by the tree roots which will inevitably try to follow up the source of moisture. Fill the box with friable soil, and go ahead and plant. The key to the success of this scheme is to regularly check the drainage holes and cut out offending tree roots as they appear.

Miniature Roses

Miniature roses add cuteness and charm to a garden in return for surprisingly little effort. At the moment, they are enjoying a wave of popularity, partly because of the number of people who are growing them in the smaller gardens of apartments and units, and also because many garden centres and stores can supply them throughout the year, propagated from cuttings at quite reasonable prices. The range of colours equals that of their larger counterparts and there is plenty of variation in their heights and effects.

Although miniatures are very easy to grow, there are a few things to bear in mind in order to get the best results from them.

Most miniatures grow to barely half a metre high, and although they grow quite well in the garden, care must be taken that they do not become overpowered by larger plants. Keep them at the front of the garden bed, perhaps concentrated near the pathway or other prominent position, so that they can be seen to best advantage. Better still, plant them in a slightly raised bed on a rockery, or in a low planter box (up to 200 mm deep is ideal).

Miniatures do better in containers than any other type of rose, as they may be moved around to catch the sun, or be brought in and out of doors for a few days at a time.

I have a particular fondness for the mini-stems (the miniatures budded onto

Sparrieshoop

the top of a half-metre stem where they form a ball of flower and foliage). These mix well with bush miniatures to achieve extra height, and they are quite distinctive when used as solitary specimen plants either in the garden or in pots.

There are several excellent climbing miniatures which can be used either as a backdrop to the bush miniatures or on their own. The smallest of the orthodox climbing roses reach 2 m or more, so the climbing miniatures fill in the size bracket from 1 to 2 m in height.

Public Gardens

The garden supervisor of a large metropolitan council once told me that, "flowers per dollar", roses are the best way of adding colour to municipal gardens. He was in a good position to make such a remark for he had planted thousands of roses throughout his domain and they were indeed a credit to his conviction.

Overseas, far more than in Australia, use is made of massed plantings of roses in public places. With a few exceptions, our efforts have been rather weak. This is surprising, indeed disappointing, considering that we enjoy such a long flowering season and a temperate climate in which to grow them. Besides this, the range of colourful and hardy roses suited for public planting is increasing each year as more roses are being bred for this purpose.

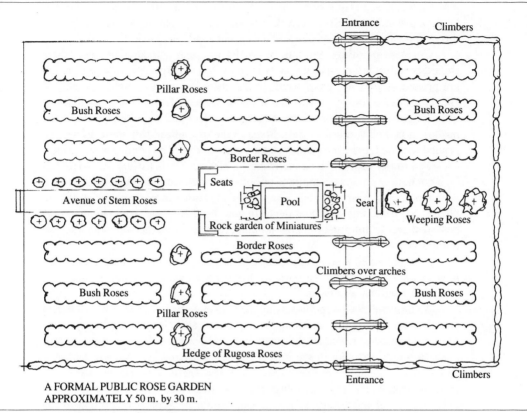

Entrance
Climbers

Pillar Roses

Bush Roses

Bush Roses

Border Roses

Seats

Avenue of Stem Roses

Pool

Seat

Weeping Roses

Rock garden of Miniatures

Border Roses

Climbers over arches

Bush Roses

Bush Roses

Pillar Roses

Hedge of Rugosa Roses

Entrance
Climbers

A FORMAL PUBLIC ROSE GARDEN
APPROXIMATELY 50 m. by 30 m.

Some of the reasons why public plantings do not always come up to expectations:

Selection of unsuitable varieties. Roses in public gardens are there for one reason; to provide maximum flowering for minimum maintenance. Exhibition roses, personal favourites and any other special-effects roses are inappropriate. There are many suitable varieties to choose from, excluding those mentioned.

Indiscriminately mixed varieties. Having chosen the ideal varieties, plant plenty of each. A whole bed or row of one variety will not look out of place; in fact, it is the best way to achieve maximum effect.

Excessive spacing. I have seen many beds spoiled because of too much space between the plants. The bushes stand like soldiers on parade, an arm's length between them. The rose bed looks mean (as if the money ran out before the job was finished) and the gardeners spend time maintaining useless ground that should be producing blooms. If resources are limited, it is best to thoroughly complete fewer beds, for it is not possible to go back and plant more roses in the gaps, but you can go on and extend the beds later.

Unsuitable siting. Public plantings are no more immune than home gardens from the problems of robbing tree roots. In addition, they often have to contend

81

with fumes, heat and dust from traffic, short-cuts through beds, reclaimed areas of land, and vandalism. Roses can do a wonderful job, but do not expect them to thrive in positions where you would not expect anything to live.

Careless pruning. We talk of cruelty to dumb animals, but surely there should be some action against cruelty to roses, too. Many public rose gardens are not pruned — they are slaughtered. If ever there is a need for lighter pruning to encourage dense, bushy growth, it is in public gardens. Lighter pruning will take a little longer but, in terms of the subsequent effect and the ultimate life of the bushes, it is well worth the effort. Some of the specialized park varieties may be pruned with hedge shears or brush cutters, and some need no pruning whatsoever.

Too many cooks. Some incredible hassles occur when every second person on a council or grounds committee or board or whatever thinks that he or she is a rose expert. The poor gardener, who most likely knows more than anyone, tries to please everyone. Put your confidence in your head gardener, equip him with the best resources, information and training, and let him get on with the job uninterrupted.

Having looked at some of the negative aspects of public plantings, let us turn now to something a bit more positive. Roses are essentially colour, so use them where they will be seen most.

A colourful, well-kept display by the main entrance to a head office, council chambers or club house, or along the approach paths, is always a lovely sight. Memorial gardens, rest areas, hospitals and rest homes are all places where people pause a while and take in the beauty of their surroundings. Modern park-like cemeteries also lend themselves to rose plantings. There, of course, you can create a grand vista, with a large sweeping expanse of rose beds nestling in the turf. Such beds can be of any imaginable size, but should be kept in proportion to the surroundings. Do not have too large a garden squeezed within the confines of a small area; nor should you have a rose bed which looks like a speck lost in an expanse of parkland.

Try introducing some extra height and points of interest by constructing arbours, pergolas and tripods for climbers. Occasional rows of stem roses will serve to emphasize an area. Banks of shrub roses will make informal backgrounds. Cluster roses are generally the most suited to massed plantings because of their freedom of flowering and their compact habit of growth.

Roses are often used as a deterrent against people taking short-cuts across gardens, and some of the shrub roses and hybrid species would stop even the most determined trespasser. Of course, the roses themselves must be protected until they reach a fair size. Breakages by romping dogs, trespassers and flying footballs can be minimized by pruning the branches of a new plant to about 150 mm at planting time and mounding extra soil over it until it becomes established. Do not leave the plant labels on at first, for theft of newly planted roses is by no means unknown.

CHAPTER TEN

The earliest roses

*History, species roses, European and
Chinese roses, influence of wild roses*

It would be very easy for a newcomer to rose-growing to imagine that the large, double, high-centred roses that are well known today have existed all along, and been picked out of the wild basically in that form. A novice probably knows the wayside briar quite well, but would not ever think that modern roses have come from anything resembling them. It is a fact, however, and it seems all the more remarkable when you trace their development from the single roses to the modern formal blooms.

Roses have been observed and plucked out of their wild state since the beginning of civilized history. They were frequently mentioned in records from the Middle East, 2000 to 3000 years ago, and were grown extensively in cultivation during the Roman era.

Currently, over one hundred distinctly different species are recorded whose natural habitats range from the Mediterranean to China, through Europe to Britain, and through the North American continent. The greatest and most divergent selection comes from temperate zones of China, suggesting that the genus may have originated in that area. On the other hand, some of the most ancient rose fossils (several over twenty million years old) have been discovered on the west side of the North American continent. The earliest records have come from the eastern Mediterranean area where the names of Syria and Rhodes both translate to "rose", and five-thousand-year-old carvings unearthed on the island of Crete clearly depict roses.

Despite its wide distribution north of the equator, the genus *Rosa* never crossed to the south, so all of the self-sown wild roses which almost overrun some parts of the countryside have been introduced since the arrival of white settlers. My ancestors took up land in the hills behind Adelaide in 1840, which was only four years after colonization, and the story goes that the men were sent along the creeks to collect briar (*R. canina*) seedlings to plant as hedges, so rapid was the adaptation of this species to its new environment.

Most of the species have simple five-petalled blossoms similar to those of their botanic cousins, the pomes, the Prunus family, the berries and the hawthorns. Some blossoms are the size of a fingernail, others are saucer-size. Most are in soft shades of cream, white or pale pink, but with some striking exceptions in bright yellow, scarlet, magenta and lilac species. In most cases the species will set colourful seed pods or hips after the spring blossoms have finished.

Being the result of rigorous natural selection and survival, the species roses were very hardy in their native environment, although, as man started to move them to foreign climates, some started to show weaknesses such as tenderness to frost and susceptibility to black spot and mildew diseases in their strange new homes.

As do other plants, roses often mutate or ''sport'' from the five-petalled single to a double form of bloom and, also as with other plants, gardeners tend to prefer the double forms, which were probably brought into the gardens as slips or cuttings (for many doubles are sterile and consequently do not set seeds and reproduce as seedlings). Colour and growth mutations also occurred, and when these were of garden value, they too became cultivated varieties.

Even before the great Roman Empire came to power, several species roses with double petals had been brought into cultivation in Greece, Crete and Asia Minor, to be later taken up by the Romans and grown extensively for cut flowers and garden plants by their aristocracy. Following the demise of the Roman Empire, roses were maintained within the monasteries, not so much for their beauty but for their reputed value for medicinal purposes. By the eighteenth century, when roses were again freely available and grown by the masses, albeit those of some means, five broad classes had emerged.

R. gallica or the Red Rose class can be traced to the earliest cultivated plants, and, as the name implies, consists mainly of red to magenta shades. Also of great antiquity is *R. damascena* or the Damask Rose which bears some likeness to the Gallicas but is mainly in tones of pink, and rather more vigorous and open in habit. *R. alba* or the White Rose class features attractive light green foliage contrasting with white or pale pink flowers, suggesting some influence from a cross with *R. canina* or the Briar Rose. *R. alba* is the national symbol of England. It is best known as the White Rose of York during the Wars of the Roses. The opposing party adopted the original Gallica (the Red Rose of Lancaster) as its emblem and, as is well known, the warring parties eventually symbolically adopted the Rose of York and Lancaster, a striped Damask rose. This was not a cross between the red and white roses as is often assumed, but an ancient part-coloured rose botanically known as *R. damascena versicolor*.

Rather more recent to appear was *R. centifolia* or Rose of a Hundred Leaves, which has, literally, a hundred petals, (not leaves, as the botanic name erroneously states). These became popularly known as Cabbage Roses. Later roses were to look even more like cabbages, and this has led to some confusion. Possibly the best-known of the early types was the Moss Rose, *R. centifolia muscosa*. The "moss" is actually enlarged glandular projections on the sepals, calyx and sometimes on the stems of the plant. It is a mutation, usually from *R. centifolia*, and consequently the flowers are very double, and in shades of white, and pink to dusky red, the same as the original Centifolia.

All five classes or groups have several features in common. They are double, fragrant, of muted colours, frost hardy and resistant to diseases. They all suffer from the disadvantages of being spring-flowering only, and rather susceptible to mildew in some climates. In order to describe them as a group representing the first major step towards the modern roses, they are generally referred to as the "Old European Roses".

During the later part of the eighteenth century, the trade routes between the East and the West were well-established and, quite naturally, some of the luxuries of the East, including some rose species, began to arrive in Europe. The Far East abounded in rose species that were varied and interesting in the extreme. Some that are known today in their original forms are *R. banksia* (Lady Banks Rose), *R. laevigata* (Cherokee Rose) and *R. gigantea*.

Other varieties which have had a profound impact on our modern roses are 'Slater's Crimson', 'Parson's Pink', 'Hume's Blush' and 'Park's Yellow'. Their colours were distinctly different, but they had several other factors in common: bright colour, glossy foliage, a light, branching habit and, most important, they flowered constantly from each of their fine, nodding stems. For rose growers accustomed to the spring-flowering European roses, this was indeed a revolution. Obligingly, these four China roses crossed readily within their group, producing many more with similar characteristics. Before many more years elapsed, the China roses had been crossed with some of the European roses, giving rise to a succession of new classes — Portlands, Noisettes, Boursalts and Bourbons — which still appear in early rose books and in the gardens of old-fashioned rose enthusiasts. The Boursalts (mainly pink) and the Portlands (mainly red) have almost disappeared, but the Noisettes (yellow to apricot blooms and of climbing habit) and the Bourbons (mainly pink shades, cabbage form and strong, upright habit) are still useful as period shrubs.

Breeding during the second half of the nineteenth century steadily developed roses that flowered twice or sometimes three times during the season, and which were more compact and hardy in growth than the China roses, which were distinctly frost tender. By the standards of those days, they seemed to be perpetually in flower, and were known as Hybrid Perpetuals, although by present day standards that term seems grossly optimistic.

Another development from the original China roses was a class with long, pointed buds, blooms that were fully double when open, almost continuous flowering, and a scent supposedly like a freshly opened tea-chest; they were thus known as Tea roses. Unfortunately, they proved too frost tender for European gardens, and they almost became extinct. Recently, however, there has grown an awareness in Australia and New Zealand of the beauty and performances of these hundred-year-old charmers and, free from the threat of frost damage, they are staging a strong comeback in the two countries.

The next development could be considered as important as the introduction of the China roses. In 1867, the hardy robustness of the Hybrid Perpetual was crossed with a floriferous, yet dainty, Tea rose, creating what was later to be known as the Hybrid Tea class. It was named 'La France' and it remained in the limelight for over half a century. At an ever accelerating rate other Hybrid Teas followed until, by the early 1900s, they dominated the popular selections of the day.

Do not think that in those early years rose breeding was a fairly uncertain process.

From the early 1800s botanists and breeders understood, albeit sketchily, the principles of cross pollination, and thousands of "different" varieties were being launched on the market. In fact, because such a limited selection of breeding source materials was available, many were practically identical and nurseries listed hundreds in their catalogues which read monotonously. Fortunately, natural selection and public demand has left us with the best of them, to enjoy as examples of the exciting early years of rose development.

You will recall that there are somewhere over one hundred distinct species, so it is interesting to note that by the turn of the century, fewer than ten had contributed to the development of cultivated roses. Obviously, there are many species with apparent features that could contribute to making better and different new varieties. Breeders were well aware of this but, in practice, it is not as easy as it sounds.

Many species will not cross with other widely differing species. For instance, the well-known *R. banksia* could contribute much by way of early flowering, healthy foliage and thornlessness, yet it is quite impossible to breed from. Some species breed quite freely, but their progeny pass on their worst characteristics, such as excessive thorniness. Also, species or varieties with differing chromosome numbers (i.e. the basic genetic chain of inheritance) might breed quite readily, but the resultant seedlings will be sterile, thus effectively preventing further development. On rare occasions, however, a chance fertile seedling may occur and the breakthrough has been achieved. One such example occurred when the bright yellow *R. foetida persiana* was finally crossed into the Hybrid Tea class, bringing with it the potential for a whole new range of colours — yellow, bronze, sunset and orange — which hitherto had been unheard of in garden roses.

Another important development took place at the turn of the century. *R. multiflora*, now best known as rootstock, was used to produce a class of roses which featured masses of tiny blooms in clusters (to be known for the next half-century as Polyantha) and which, when crossed with the better-known Hybrid Teas, produced a class with medium-sized blooms in moderate clusters, and a hardy, low to medium habit. This class swept onto the rose scene under the name of Floribunda.

R. wichuraiana (Memorial Rose) is another species which played a significant role. It is a strong, completely prostrate rambler which has an influence on

DEVELOPMENT OF THE ROSE THROUGH THE AGES

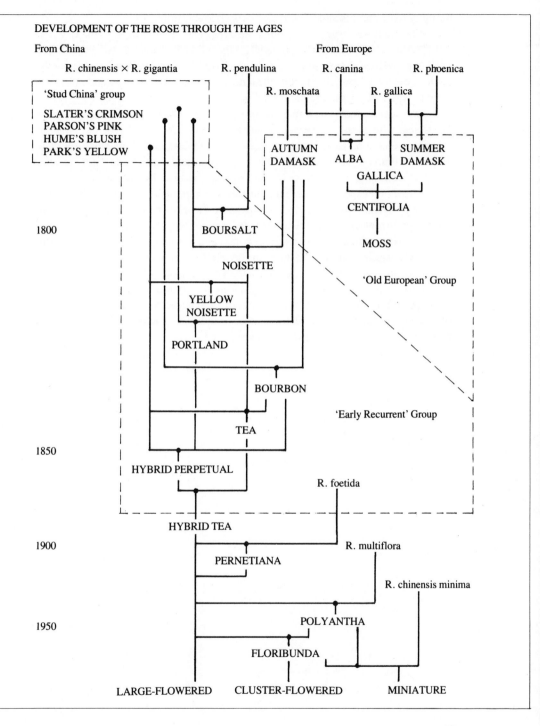

many of the ramblers and natural climbers up to this time.

Nor must we forget *R. gigantea*, an evergreen rambler from southern China which Australia's best-known breeder, Alister Clark, used extensively to create such winter-flowering roses as 'Lorraine Lee' and 'Nancy Hayward'. Regrettably, besides the ever-flowering factor, the tendency to powdery mildew and rather soft growth was carried into the breeding line.

One species that is now making an ever increasing impact on the rose world is the tiniest rose of all, *R. chinensis minima*, which since the 1930s has been the major influence on the Miniature class. Not only are its flowers small (perhaps 30 mm in diameter) but the whole plant — leaves, stems, prickles — is also scaled down accordingly. You will see this same petite charm in the miniatures of today.

A few other species have had moments of popularity, but eventually led into a breeding "cul-de-sac". *R. rugosa* (Japanese Rose) was used to produce some hardy, recurrent and fragrant bushes; *R. macrantha* produced a small group of strong bushes with exquisite single blooms; and *R. spinosissima* (Scotch Burnet Rose) was used extensively last century to produce some ferny, but spiny, bushes which featured purple to lilac blooms and interesting black hips.

One particularly useful class of roses are the Hybrid Musks. They typify the concept of a true shrub rose — strong, hardy and attractive plants bearing masses of informal blooms throughout the season — and, consequently, they are still used extensively by rose landscaping enthusiasts.

Massed bed of 'Kalinka' reproducing an old style setting at Rippon Lea, Melbourne.

Successful use of roses for median strip planting. 'Friesia' at Ballarat, Victoria.

A mixed but well graded display of cluster flowered roses at the entrance to Ashford Community Hospital.

A small, well planned and well maintained rose feature in a suburban back garden.

(Top left)   'MRS FOLEY HOBBS' Several Tea roses such as this produce classic shaped buds which develop to the 'old world' style bloom when fully opened.

(Top right)   'DAINTY BESS' One of the best loved single flowers, it is still popular after 60 years (1925).

(Bottom left)   'LA FRANCE' Generally accepted as the original Hybrid Tea rose (1867) it paved the way to the modern large flowered varieties.

(Bottom right)   'BOULE DE NEIGE' The blooms are like snowball

CHAPTER ELEVEN

The Fascinating Old-world Roses

Earliest cultivated roses, early recurrent roses, nostalgia roses

Modern roses, without doubt, have reached an incredibly high plateau not far from perfection. Their freedom of flowering, range and brilliance of colour, excellence of blooms and hardiness of growth habit are such that it is hard to imagine how they may be improved.

Despite this near-perfection, over the past few years there has been a strong renewal of interest in the roses of earlier times. People who seek out and grow the gems of the past do so in the full knowledge that they have their weaknesses, and that in many ways they cannot be compared to the moderns. Nevertheless, they grow them, and not in ones and twos, but in gardens wholly devoted to them. As one who is equally involved with the old and the new, I ask myself why this is happening.

More people than ever are travelling overseas and seeing the old-world roses growing in the older countries, as indeed they have been growing for many years, but that should only be a stimulus to the trend rather than the reason for it. The current interest in restoring things of the past, including cars, houses and gardens, must have an influence; when you authentically restore a building, obviously it is desirable to create a garden appropriate to the architectural era. Also, there is a host of interesting variations amongst the early roses. Firstly there are the simple wild roses, then the early European roses, the cabbage-like Bourbons and the Hybrid Perpetuals; there are the fragile Chinas and Tea roses, and the several excursions into the species hybrids. Each reflects some distinctive characteristics of its parents. I think that a strong interest in old-world roses is, in many cases, a reaction, conscious or unconscious against the monotonous near-perfection of the modern roses. The old colours are more muted, more like the paintings of the old masters, and the growth is more unruly, like a busy cottage garden. They may flower only once a year, but the memory of the past spring and the eager anticipation of the season to come means that they are vivid in your mind throughout the year. The fragrance is strong and pure, with additional fragrance in the foliage and stems of some species and, for good measure, many species finish the season with a colourful display of autumn-tinted foliage and brightly coloured seed hips.

My experience, gained from advising potential growers of old-world roses, indicates that they are cultivated for many reasons. Sometimes the interested grower becomes terribly confused when confronted by the full range, so I find it helpful and logical to consider them under the following headings:

Earliest Cultivated Roses; Early Recurrent Roses; Nostalgia Roses; Climbers and Ramblers; Hybrid Species and Hardy Shrubs; Original Species; Botanic Curiosities; Historic Roses; and Authentic Plants for Old Restored Gardens. As we consider each group, the picture will become clearer.

Earliest Cultivated Roses

The "Old European Roses" are examples of the earliest roses to be grown in cultivation. They usually feature flat compact blooms which are perfectly circular in outline, with curiously ruffled and quartered petals, and some show a characteristic button-formation of the central petals. The colours, which range from white through pink to crimson and magenta, are of muted or dusky tones, and all are distinctly fragrant. The plants are of medium size, and thickety in the case of the Gallicas; rather taller in the Damasks and Albas, while the Centifolias and Mosses tend to be rather lanky and spreading. All are very resistant to frost damage and black spot fungus. They flower on masses of short stems in the late spring, but only a few repeat in the autumn. Amongst the best varieties of the dozens that have been brought back into cultivation are:

Gallicas:
Assemblage des Beautes has tight ruffled blooms of surprisingly bright crimson.

Cardinal Richelieu, which is a very deep violet-purple with silver on the reverse of the petals.

Charles de Mills, which has very large blooms of cerise-crimson.

Duchesse de Montebello, which has beautifully formed blooms of clear soft pink.

Jenny Duval has unusual and changeable colours of deep lilac-pink to grey-lavender to cerise.

Damasks:
Celsiana, which has large but delicately loose blooms of soft pink, revealing soft yellow stamens upon opening.

Ispahan is of traditional form, with tight reflexing blooms of clear pink featuring the distinctive button-eye.

Mme Hardy, which is generally considered to be one of the most beautifully formed old roses, its pure white blooms contrasting with a small green eye.

'SCABROSA'

Trigintipetala, a rather loose, medium-sized pink borne on a large bush. It is noted as a source of rose attar for perfume, hence its alternative name, 'Kazanlik', after the district in Bulgaria where it is grown for this purpose.

R. damascena versicolor is a parti-coloured species like 'Trigintipetala'. It bears random areas of pink and white, and is better-known as 'York and Lancaster' as a symbol of reunion after the English Wars of the Roses.

Albas:

Celeste (or Celestial), which is quite heavenly, with delicately loose, very pale pink blooms.

Konigin von Danemark, has large double blooms of delicate salmon pink, first cupped then opening to reflex and quarter.

Mme Plantier, which, although not a typical Alba, warrants mention for its masses of pure white, tightly formed blooms and its thick, gracefully arching habit of growth.

Centifolias:

The original *R. centifolia* (Cabbage Rose) is an excellent example, with its large, perfectly circular formation enclosing the ruffled inner petals. Its colour is clear rose pink. One variation of the pink form features a curious cresting growth of the sepals, like a cockaded hat, hence the picturesque name of **Chapeau de Napoleon** or 'Napoleon's Hat'. Another variation is the interesting crinkled foliage known as **Bullata** or the 'Lettuce-leaf Rose'. **Fantin-Latour** is a soft pink of rather more compact habit. **Tour de Malakoff** is an example of the deeper colourings. It is silver-lilac in the bud and opens to reveal mauve ageing magenta.

Moss Roses:

This is the best-known group, although they are not ideal garden plants. The name arises from the curious moss-like hairs that grow from the calyx and stems of the flowers (chance mutations from the centifolias in most cases and thus they have the same fully double rosette blooms, and the same rather open arching habit of growth).

R. centifolia muscosa (Common Moss) is the original and still one of the best, with rich mid-pink blooms. The white form, *R. centifolia muscosa alba* (more easily remembered as 'Shailer's White Moss'), is a good white example, as is **Comtesse de Murinais**. The heaviest mossing of all of the class is **Japonica** or 'Mousseaux de Japon', although the pink blooms are rather fleeting. **Henri Martin** is an excellent light red, while **William Lobb**, sometimes known as 'Old Velvet', is one of the deep crimson-purple that characterize the old-world scene. Two Moss roses which sported from the Damask group and not the Centifolias are the white **Quatre Saison Blanc Mousseux** and the purple-maroon **Deuil de Paul Fontaine**. They are slightly recurrent, but the growth habit is rather more stiff, with more bristly moss.

Quatre Saisons

Early Recurrent Roses

This group lies midway between the earliest cultivated varieties and the modern roses. The introduction of the perpetual-flowering China roses into the breeding lines gave rise to several different classes of roses that repeated flowering to varying degrees throughout the year but retained much of the distinctive old form in their blooms. They are an ideal starting point for anyone who is new to the old-rose world, but, as their forms and growth habits vary quite considerably, it would be well to bear some of these points in mind.

The **Bourbons** are one of the most popular groups. They have very double, almost globular blooms in shades of white and pink, borne on long semi-climbing canes. They can be trained as tall (2 m or more), free-standing shrubs, or as pillar roses or small climbers covering 2 or 3 m of trellis. **La Reine Victoria** is, quite deservedly, the best-known Bourbon, with almost completely globular blooms of clear pink. Its paler sport, **Mme Pierre Oger**, commences as delicate ivory, deepening wherever the petals are exposed to the sun, thus creating one of the most subtle shading effects imaginable. Several consistently striped varieties are available but **Variegata di Bologna**, with globular crimson-and-white striped blooms is possibly the best. **Mme Isaac Periere** has rather more flattish blooms of deep carmine pink, and **Boule de Neige** is an especially free-flowering white.

Finally, I must mention **Souvenir de la Malmaison**. Its huge, double, perfectly formed cup-shaped blooms of the most soft blush-cream are richly fragrant and borne almost throughout the year, but the short, sporadic growth is enough to test the patience of any nurseryman. Healthy? Yes, but impossible to propagate in sufficient quantities to meet the almost insatiable public demand for this gem.

The **Hybrid Perpetuals** produce large very double blooms that are flat, ruffled, and very fragrant almost without exception, on bushes that are more compact and sturdy than the Bourbons. Many are usually thornless. The "perpetual" part of their title is rather hopeful for they flower only sporadically after the spring flush. Their blooms range from pink to red to mauve.

Reine des Violettes has large rich velvet-purple blooms with a silver-purple reverse which shows in the characteristic button-eye.

Paul Neyron produces very large blooms of rose pink, on stout upright stems, and has often been mistakenly referred to as the Cabbage Rose, such is the size and shape of the blooms.

Mrs John Laing is a lighter pink, while **Frau Karl Druschki** (alias 'Snow Queen' during World War I) is purest white, but, alas, without perfume. **Roger Lambelin** is known best for the distinctive white margins to each of its crimson petals.

The **Tea Roses** are rapidly becoming a significant group, quite different to the Bourbons and Hybrid Perpetuals. Their blooms are rather more "modern" looking, especially in the bud stage, although the open blooms reveal the lovely "old" ruffled centres. The bushes are of average size (1.5–2 m tall), with a fine twiggy habit and thin nodding stems giving the blooms a casual cascading appearance.

The European winters were too severe for the Teas, so they never became a significant group there, but they thrive in all but the coldest Australian winters. In fact, they flower happily throughout the year until given a light pruning (which is all that they require).

Lady Hillingdon, with its lovely old-gold blooms, is one of the best-known of the class, especially in its climbing form.

General Gallieni features the curious effect found so often in the Tea roses, where the colour changes from biscuit-buff in the centre to coppery red on opening.

Papa Gontier and **Monsieur Tillier** are examples of clear rich pinks, while **Francis Dubruiel** is one of the deepest reds of any rose.

Duchesse de Brabant (sometimes known as 'Comtesse de Labarthe') is a soft pearly pink, while **Mrs Herbert Stevens** and **Niphetos** are pure white.

Safrano produces masses of rather loose saffron to apricot blooms.

Lorraine Lee which, surprisingly, is a latter-day Tea rose, produces pink flowers.

The **China Roses** cover a rather mixed selection. They are mostly quite small in habit, twiggy but nicely bushy in form, with an almost neverending sprinkling of small to medium blooms. The blooms vary in form from globular doubles to semi-singles, and in colour from white, pink, and apricot-biscuit to red.

Two of the original China roses, the crimson *R. chinensis semperflorens* and the pink **Old Blush** are examples of the casual little roses that never stop flowering.

The curious *R. chinensis viridiflora* (Chinese Green Rose) is another reliable performer which is useful as a garden display as well as for floral arrangements.

The little sweetheart, **Cecile Brunner**, needs no introduction, with its button-hole blooms of pink.

Perle d'Or is similar to 'Cecile Brunner', but bears apricot-yellow blooms.

Hermosa could well be likened to the half-sized 'La Reine Victoria' and it, together with the crimson **Fabvier** and the rose-to-crimson-coloured **Archduke Charles**, is well suited for front row plantings.

The early Hybrid Tea roses produce blooms which feature the old globular form in most cases, although several now resemble the modern habit.

La France, the original Hybrid Tea in 1867, **Lady Mary Fitzwilliam**, and **Mrs Wakefield Christie-Miller** are three examples that still remain in many collections of old roses.

Nostalgia Roses

I have been approached many times with enquiries about 'old-world' roses such as 'Talisman', 'Crimson Glory', 'Comtesse Vandal', and 'Shot Silk'. It is too easy to be smug and to ridicule someone who is taking his or her first tentative steps into the world of old roses and, often, I must admit, my first impulse is to say haughtily that they are positively modern compared to my collection. These folks are seeking roses that they knew in their youth, perhaps in their sweetheart days or as their first home-and-garden roses.

There is an obvious interest in and demand for these roses, which I have decided to call the nostalgia roses. Very approximately they span the period between the World Wars and, as it is not possible to mention them all, the following is a list of those which come repeatedly to my attention:

(Red)
'Crimson Glory'; 'Daily Mail Scented'; 'Hadley'; 'Texas Centennial'.
(Pink)
'Comtesse Vandal'; 'Dame Edith Helen'; 'Ophelia'; 'Radiance'; 'Shot Silk'.
(Autumn tones)
'Mevrou G. A. Rossem'; 'President Herbert Hoover'; 'Talisman'.
(Yellow)
'Golden Dawn'; 'Golden Ophelia'; 'Mme Pierre Du Pont'.
(Hybrid Polyanthas)
'Orange Triumph'; 'Permanent Wave'; and many Poulsen varieties.

Although the memories of these are still strong, it is often a little disappointing to see them again and to realize that at least some of them do not stand comparison with their more recent alternatives. Nevertheless, some enthusiasts are maintaining the nostalgia roses for posterity.

Climbers and Ramblers

Climbers and ramblers are discussed fully in other parts of the book, but the species and early cultivated climbers must be included in this discussion about old-world roses too.

In general, the old-world climbers and ramblers exhibit the extremes of their type. There are the massive growers, e.g., *R. banksia*, (Lady Banks Rose), *R. laevigata* (Cherokee Rose) and *R. filipes*; those of completely prostrate habit, e.g. *R. wichuraiana* (Memorial Rose) and *R. bracteata* (Macartney Rose); and the hardy 'Mermaid'. The tiny blooms of *R. banksia* and *R. multiflora*, the large blooms of *R. laevigata* (Cherokee Rose) and *R. gigantea*, the scent of *R. wichuraiana* and *R. moschata*, the unusual colours of 'Fortune's Double Yellow' and 'Veilchenbleu' (violet-blue), and the display of autumn hips of *R. brunonii* (Himalayan Musk) and 'Wedding Day' all bear witness to the wide-ranging virtues of old-world climbers and ramblers.

Many of the old bush roses are available in climbing form too. Their large globular or cup-shaped, nodding blooms blend well with their bush-growing counterparts and are useful for adding extra height or screening to the landscape.

The older climbers are generally informal and thus look fine rambling over old buildings, sheds or ruins, climbing through dead tree-trunks, cascading over embankments and even being allowed to grow over themselves as an ever expanding mound supported only by their own growth beneath (a wonderful effect when space is not limited).

Here are some of the most popular and useful climbers:

R. banksia (Lady Banks Rose), one of the best-known and best-loved climbers, possibly because of its very early display of tiny yellow or white blossoms borne in clusters along the length of all of its slim branches, and because of its smooth, thornless growth. It is easy to train, yet can be allowed to develop into a huge plant.

R. laevigata (Cherokee Rose), sometimes known as *R. sinica alba* or 'White Macartney', is another very early spring bloomer. It has exquisitely formed, large white single blooms borne against a backdrop of glossy green, almost evergreen, foliage.

R. bracteata (Macartney Rose) bears ivory white single blooms with a large and distinctive centre of golden stamens. The growth is low and spreading, and extremely hardy, even if rather thorny. The highly regarded hybrid, **Mermaid** is a constant favourite, with large single yellow blooms in compact little clusters appearing steadily throughout the year. Being quite vigorous and thorny it can only be recommended for larger areas.

Several climbers feature masses of small single blooms. **Wedding Day** is one of the favourites. Its creamy white little blooms feature distinctive orange-yellow stamens, followed by a crop of small red hips in autumn, and the foliage is large, thick and glossy.

R. brunonii (Himalayan Musk) has airy panicles of strongly scented creamy blooms, followed by a display of small orange hips borne in a similar open, airy formation.

Felicite et Perpetue is an example of a double white, with pompons borne on a vigorous but lax-growing rambler that likes nothing better than to scramble through the branches of the tallest trees.

Fortune's Double Yellow, sometimes known as 'Beauty of Glazenwood', enjoys a dazzling couple of weeks in early spring, with decorative blooms of amber-orange flashed with crimson. It qualifies for the name "yellow" because in its time it was the closest to yellow of any climber — how things have changed.

R. wichuraiana, sometimes known as the 'Memorial Rose', is a completely lax, ground hugging rambler with delicious apple-scented little white blooms. It is ideal as a true cascading ground cover. (I have known people who "prune" theirs with a grass mower.) More importantly, it is the parent of many well-known ramblers, the best known of which is the little pink **Dorothy Perkins** — absolutely ideal for trailing over arches and pergolas, although rather prone to mildew in some climates.

Albertine is another *R. wichuraiana* hybrid, and it can be found rambling over many an English cottage. The large double blooms are a distinctive coppery chamois colour and richly perfumed, while the growth is stout and vigorous.

Bloomfield Courage, has single bright scarlet blooms and a distinctive white eye, and is ideal for introducing some stronger colour into the garden.

Veilchenbleu is a smaller climber which, as the name states, is one of the bluest roses of all, especially in the cooler weather or in partial shade.

The Noisette class of roses lie somewhere near the Tea roses and the Bourbons, except that these roses are either climbing or shrub-climbing in habit. They nevertheless include some very beautiful specimens.

Jaune Desprez is large, double and fragrant, with apricot-pink blooms on a small climber.

Lamarque has smallish but nicely formed creamy white blooms in nodding clusters on an almost thornless soft matt green climber.

Gloire de Dijon bears large, double, nodding Tea roses of rich buff-pink, making it one of the most sought-after of its type.

The climbing form of the Tea rose **Devoniensis** makes a strong ever-blooming display of soft apricot and, like all of the class, is very fragrant.

The beautiful soft pink **Souvenir de la Malmaison** is available in climbing habit with huge, exquisitely cupped blooms borne for most of the year.

Zephirine Drouhin is useful for a number of reasons. It is rich cerise-pink (a good contrast against many of the paler tones), the flowers are dainty and nicely pointed, and the foliage is attractively tinged copper and completely thornless. Although classed as a Bourbon, it shares few similarities, but is a most useful climber.

Species and Close Hybrids

Many of the original species and their close hybrids are grown for garden display. I have already mentioned the climbing species, but there are many more that make interesting and worthwhile landscaping effects.

We cannot generalize about the effects because they vary to extremes — some are fine, twiggy growers with airy, fern-like foliage such as the bright yellow *R. ecae*, some feature brilliant blossoms and equally spectacular hips like the *R. moyesii* group, others feature huge single blooms with open arching growth (*R. macrantha* types), while the well-known *R. rugosa* are noted for their thick leathery foliage, compact habit, large blooms and large fruity hips.

Most of this group have been brought direct from their wild habitat, although an increasing number of especially selected hybrids are being used, thus making them even more suited for garden displays.

'Golden Chersonese' has the brilliant yellow of its parent, *R. ecae*, and has more robust growth. *R. moyesii* 'Geranium' is a more compact form of the parent, so it is ideally suited to smaller gardens. 'Nevada' is another *R. moyesii* hybrid. It makes a thicker, more recurrent shrub and, mercifully it is almost thornless. 'Carmenetta' retains much of the reddish foliage and stems of its parent, *R. rubrifolia*, but has bigger and more elegant flowers.

It is unfortunate that many gardeners immediately associate the species with the wild briars that dot the roadsides, as they would be one of the least elegant species, noted mainly for their masses of little orange hips and their aromatic foliage (hence the name 'Sweet Briar').

The species have three qualities which commend their use. Firstly, they are hardy informal shrubs which come in many shapes, sizes and effects. They make an easy transition from the formal rose types to the native garden, or indeed the natural shrubland. Being stronger and less demanding than formal roses, they can rely primarily on winter and spring rains to bring on the late spring flowering, after which they will survive on intermittent watering. Pruning and maintenance requirements are minimal — only light trimming after flowering and thinning when necessary. They are naturally trouble free, requiring spraying only during extreme conditions and heavy infestations. Secondly, whole stems of blossoms may be cut for floral arrangements, and the clusters of autumn hips and the autumn foliage on many make a long-lasting display. Thirdly, the species are living illustrations of the origins of modern roses. It is interesting to compare the attributes of the original with how it has been bred into the successive generations of its progeny, and to reflect on what has been achieved by rose breeding — the real improvements and those which are only cosmetic.

Some species which are well worth growing:

Rugosa group (Japanese Rose). Thick, compact habit to 1.5 m; very healthy thick leathery foliage; flower recurrently in ruby red to lilac to white; hips are large and round.

Blanc Double de Coubert. Double white blooms.

Frau Dagmar Hastrup. Low, spreading, single lilac blooms and red hips.

Roseraie de l'Hay. Double purple peony-like blooms.

R. rugosa alba. Large single white blooms and a heavy crop of hips.

R. rugosa scabrosa. (usually known as 'Scabrosa'). First choice; large single purple blooms and large red hips.

Schneezwerg (Snow Dwarf). Small, neat, anemone-like white blooms and red hips.

Pimpinellifoliae group (which is simply a way of saying they feature small ferny-like foliage). The blooms are usually white to yellow, borne closely along the twiggy bronzy red branches; flower early in spring; 1-2 m tall.

Canary Bird. Large single yellow that give some repeat blooms.

R. ecae. Small brilliant yellow blooms; attractively shrubby habit.

R. foetida bicolor (Austria Copper). Spectacular bi-colour; nasturtium red blooms with straw yellow reverse.

R. harisonii (Harison's Rose). Cupped, double blooms of clear yellow.

R. primula (Incense Rose). Soft single yellow blooms which give a distinct incense scent when the soft tips are bruised.

R. sericea pteracantha (Maltese Cross Rose). Ivory white blooms; a unique rose with only four petals, hence the common name; features enormous, yet attractive, red thorns.

Cinnamomeae group. Usually features smooth cinnamon coloured wood and single blooms of white through cinnamon-pink to purple and red, followed by distinctive flagon-shaped or elongated hips.

R. fedtschenkoana. Large attractive shrub to 2 m; has grey-green foliage and amethyst-red growing tips; recurrent single white blooms and red hips.

R. moyesii. Brilliant red single blooms with spectacular orange hips.

100

R. moyesii **Geranium.** More compact version of the original *R. moyesii*.

Nevada. Large, almost single creamy white blooms, slightly tipped crimson; recurrent and almost thornless; large, spreading but tidy shrub.

Marguerite Hilling. Carmine-pink variation of Nevada.

R. wardii culta. Virtually a white *R. moyesii* with golden stamens.

Caninae group. Variable; usually with open, briar-like habit.

Carmenetta. Dainty little lilac blooms and distinctly bronze-red foliage and stems.

R. eglanteria (or *R. rubiginosa*). Noted for the characteristic sweet aroma from the foliage.

Finally we have examples from various other groups or sub-genera:

R. hardii. Quaint little yellow blooms with a bright red zone at the base of each petal; fine twiggy grower of small size.

R. roxburghii plena (Chestnut Rose or Burr Rose). An unusual species with quite attractive double blooms in light pink tones; the buds are heavily "burred", and the glossy green foliage forms a dense cover on the large, spreading plant.

R. stellata mirifica. Large lilac blooms and bristling hips; unusual grey gooseberry-like foliage.

R. virginiana. Moderate shrub with especially attractive foliage, and masses of small red hips in autumn.

Hardy Shrubs and Hybrid Species

There are many excellent roses which are difficult to define.

I suppose you could say that all roses are shrubs, but some cannot be further classified accurately as modern (even if they are quite recent), species or old world. They might be characterized as informal growers which have hardy constitutions and which flower in masses, or in clusters of small decorative blooms, but it would be a general description only.

Like species roses, shrub roses blend well with other shrubs either as massed plantings or as selected specimen plants. Generally, they grow to between 1.5 m and 2.5 m high and, often, up to the same spread. They may be cut as large branches and used for softening the edges of traditional (or modern) floral arrangements, and they are useful in backgrounds too.

Some of the best and most interesting of the group:

Ballerina. Large heads of small single blooms edged carmine; flowers throughout the season; easy, arching habit which is not too large.

Bloomfield Abundance. Virtually a shrub-growing form of the old favourite 'Cecile Brunner' (the little pink button-hole rose).

Buff Beauty. Large pompons of apricot-buff; delightfully fragrant; cascading habit.

Cornelia. Dainty, cascading blooms of soft apricot-pink; almost thornless; semi-weeping habit.

Elmshorn. Masses of small deep pink to red pompons.

Felicia. Similar to Penelope but with apricot-pink blooms.

Fruhlingsgold. Similar to Fruhlingsmorgen except that the blooms are soft gold and semi-single.

Fruhlingsmorgen (Spring Morn). Refreshing, large single cream edged rose pink blooms on a large, thickety bush.

Penelope. Shapely little blooms of soft shell pink; very fragrant.

Sea Foam. Variously catalogued as a Floribunda, a climber or a ground cover; bears clusters of double white blooms on growth that arches along the ground in a series of short hops; easily trained upwards, outwards or down.

Yesterday. Large sprays of dainty lilac-pink blooms (like 'Ballerina').

Botanic Curiosities

There is no doubt that many folk, when they first come upon the old-world roses, are amazed and intrigued by some of the curiosities that abound amongst them. A few may seem rather gimmicky, but they serve as examples of the endless evolutionary offshoots of nature, and some turn out to be worthwhile and attractive variations.

The first time that the simple five-petalled rose sported or mutated into the double form it must have created considerable interest amongst our forebears of centuries ago.

The mossing effect that occurs on Centifolias is another curiosity that became accepted and, indeed, highly sought after as a new strain of rose — the Moss rose. This can be seen at its extreme in the variety '**Japonica**'. Some variations are grotesque, as in the crested sepals of 'Crested Moss' (the alternative name for '**Chapeau de Napoleon**'), the lettuce leaf effect of the centifolia, '**Bullata**', and the thick elongated maple-like leaves of *R. multiflora watsoniana*, a mutation from *R. multiflora*.

The 'Chinese Green Rose', *R. viridiflora* flowers and grows like any modern cluster rose, but its "flowers" are masses of green sepals which last for a long time and finally turn bronze before they fall. It is much sought after by floral artists.

The huge, translucent red thorns on the spring growth of *R. sericea pteracantha* make it a formidable but attractive sight.

R. stellata mirifica (Sacramento Rose), from south-western U.S.A., looks more like a gooseberry than a rose, because of its spined green hips.

R. roxburghii (Chestnut Rose) has burred hips, twin upward-facing thorns beside each leaf, and peeling bark.

R. hardii is noted particularly for its distinctive yellow blooms with a strong red splash at the base of each petal.

The hybrids, '**Fimbriata**', '**Pink Grootendorst**' and '**F.G. Grootendorst**' are unusual because their petals have fimbriate (fringed) edges which make them look for all the world like carnations.

Many striped roses occur amongst the old-world selections, but none is as well known as *R. damascena versicolor* (York and Lancaster), which bears random combinations of pink and white — sometimes whole petals, or half of the bloom, are divided into the two colours.

R. multiflora (white) or the lilac-pink *R. farreri persetosa* (Threepenny Bit Rose) produce the smallest rose blooms, and *R. chinensis minima* (scarcely 300 mm tall) is the smallest flower-and-plant combination. *R. banksia* (yellow and white) also produces very small blossoms but, if allowed to develop unchecked, can grow to be amongst the largest of all climbers.

The Rugosa species with their lovely leathery foliage and huge round hips, almost rank as curiosities.

Historic Roses

Many people are fascinated by the historical significance of various roses.

It is easy to arrange a collection of old-world roses in a way that shows the chronological development of the genus *Rosa*. The addition of suitable notes to the plant labels makes a garden enthralling for anyone who is interested in the roses' history.

For instance, the collection could start with the *R. damascena bifera* (Quatre Saison or Four Seasons Damask), a recurrent flowering pink well known in Roman times; the original spring Damask, *R. damascena trigintipetala*, which is still grown to this day in Kazanlik, Bulgaria, for the production of rose attar; and the earliest gallica, *R. gallica officinalis*, which is a light red in colour. By the seventeenth century, the traditional English rose (the *R. alba*) had been brought into cultivation and known variously as the 'White Rose of York', the 'Jacobite Rose' and 'Bonnie Prince Charlie's Rose'. These were followed closely by the Cabbage Rose (*R. centifolia*), which was a large ruffled-pink variety. By the eighteenth century, the Common Moss (*R. centifolia muscosa*) had paved the way for many of the moss variety.

In the late 1700s, explorers from the Far East brought back the revolutionary China roses, which so radically changed rose breeding over the next century. Three of these still remain — 'Slater's Crimson' (*R. chinensis semperflorens*) a delicate little crimson variety, 'Old Bush' (or Parson's Pink) a semi-single pink; and 'Rouletti', (*R. chinensis minima*) the parent of the miniature class. The vigorous climbing cream-white variety, *R. gigantea*, was also to become, through the work of Australian breeder Alister Clark, one of the important varieties used in rose breeding.

During the "heady" days of rose breeding, in the late 1800s and early 1900s, *R. multiflora*, *R. wichuraiana*, *R. moschata* and *R. foetida persiana* were all to make very important contributions to the development of our modern roses. These varieties can still be found today, growing as living examples of the ancestors of our modern rose.

Champney's Pink Cluster is generally accepted as the original Noisette rose, while **Rose Edouard** and **Bourbon Queen** (Reine des Iles Bourbon) mark the beginning of the important Bourbon class.

La France is traditionally regarded as the first Hybrid Tea, the longest lasting and most important class in rose history; while **Soliel d'Or** (1900) marked the introduction of the bright yellows and orange colourings of the class that was to

Champney's Pink Cluster

become known as Pernetianas. **Lady Mary Fitzwilliam** (1882), possibly the most prolific parent of all roses, was thought to be extinct, but only recently it has been rediscovered and has become a coveted collector's plant.

Mignonette (1880) represents the beginning of the Polyantha class, while **Orleans Rose** (1909) was the first of what were to become the Orleans Polyanthas.

Authentic Garden Restorations

Many people are now taking an interest in the old-world, or heritage, roses with a view to incorporating them into an "old garden" restoration (this may be in a private garden, but more often it is for the garden of a public building or a National Trust property). The success of such a project is determined by the care and detail of the research that is undertaken, not just by the funds that are available. Lists of plants that were grown in the garden at the time are not now available. However, local records may help. Long-established nurseries may still have catalogues from that era, or the Public Library or Archives of the appropriate State's capital, or more especially, the library of the Botanic Garden may have such catalogues. The next step would be to study the books and journals covering the period, especially descriptions of particularly notable gardens of the time, such as the records that are still available from Elizabeth Bay House in Sydney.

The Heritage Rose groups, both of Australia and New Zealand, should be able to help, as will the garden section of the National Trust. Of course, very few varieties of these roses would still be available now, but you should, at least, be able to obtain varieties that are still quite authentic and in keeping with the period.

However, we do know that some roses have remained in commercial production throughout the period since their introduction. For instance, the 'Yellow Banksia' (*R. banksia lutea*) is still as popular today as it ever was. *R. laevigata* is another species that can still be found climbing over old buildings, although perhaps it is better known by its Australian adopted names of 'White Macartney' or *R. sinica alba*. The pink hybrid *R. anemonoides*, again better known in Australia as 'Pink Macartney' or *R. sinica anemone* is also still available. A close relative is *R. fortuniana*, a white double, which was a favourite for trailing over summer-houses, sheds and other obviously Australian outhouses. '**Dorothy Perkins**' enjoyed great popularity early this century, while '**Hiawatha**' and '**Bloomfield Courage**' were other varieties of the true rambling types. '**Fortune's Double Yellow**' provided early spring colour, and the white '**Felicite et Perpetue**' (known also at times as the 'Guildford Briar') was often found clinging to the topmost branches of dead trees. '**Mermaid**' (1918) was a later arrival which climbed onwards regardless of utter neglect, as did its parent *R. bracteata*, the true 'Macartney Rose', which preferred to scramble along the ground.

Turning to the bush and shrub varieties, who has not failed to notice the wild briars that thrive along roads and creeks throughout parts of Australia? These are either a form of *R. canina* or, those with aromatic foliage are a form of *R. eglanteria*. Bear in mind that these were often planted as hedgerows by the early settlers. Since the earliest days, the blush pink *R. indica major* was used as a nursery understock, and many reverted to suckering, over-running the intended variety and then becoming a substantial display in their own right in the early spring. To a lesser extent, this also happened with the understock 'Ragged Robin', more correctly called '**Gloire des Rosomanes**', with its light crimson blooms.

A few of the early European roses which were known to be grown in early gardens were '**Quatre Saison**' (the Autumn Damask) and '**Trigintipetala**' (the Spring Damask), the *R. centifolia muscoas alba* under the name of 'White Bath', the 'Common Moss' (*R. centifolia muscosa*), and the 'York and Lancaster' (*R. damascena versicolor*). Smaller growing varieties that were also found were '**Charles de Mills**' (crimson), '**Tour de Malakoff**' (magenta), and 'Rosa Mundi' (*R. gallica versicolor*).

Among the more recent roses, referred to earlier (page 95) under the heading "Early Recurrent Roses" were the Noisettes '**Lamarque**' (1830), '**Cloth of Gold**' (1843), and '**Alister Stella Gray**' (1894); the Bourbons '**Boule de Neige**' (1867), '**Mme Isaac Periere**' (1881), '**La Reine Victoria**' (1872), and the climber '**Zephirine Drouhin**' (1868); and the Hybrid Perpetuals '**Paul Neyron**'

(1869), '**Prince Camille de Rohan**' (1861), '**Roger Lambelin**' (1890), and '**Frau Karl Druschki**' (1901).

The Tea roses and early Hybrid Teas, however, provide some of the best restoration varieties for use, as they are free with their blooms, moderate in size and truly characterize the "turn of the century" gardens.

The Tea roses, (with their nodding heads, pointed buds and ruffled blooms when open), could be represented by '**General Gallieni**' (1899), '**Maman Cochet**' (1893), '**Duchesse de Brabant**' (or 'Comtesse de Labarthe'), '**Hugo Roller**' (1907), '**Lady Hillingdon**' (1910), '**Safrano**' (1839), and '**Mrs Herbert Stevens**' (1910).

Some early Hybrid Tea varieties would be '**La France**' (1867), '**Mrs Wakefield Christie-Miller**' (1909), and '**Mme Abel Chatenay**' (1895).

Finally, we must not forget the little China and Polyanthas roses. '**Cecile Brunner**' has been a continuous favourite since it was introduced in 1882, supported by its apricot-yellow counterpart '**Perle d'Or**' (1884). '**Old Blush**' (sometimes called the 'Pink Monthly') was quite common, while, for lower plantings, '**Cramoisi Superieur**' (1832) would have been used.

Cecile Brunner

(Top left)   'VARIEGATA DI BOLOGNA' One of the Bourbon class from 1909 with one of the best striped effects to be found on any rose.

(Top right)   'CHARLES DE MILLS' is a later Gallica with more double, perfectly formed blooms.

(Centre left)   'CREPUSCULE' An early Noisette class, which makes a thick cascading mound of buff-yellow blooms.

(Centre right) R. alba semi-plena or 'Bonnie Prince Charlies' rose is intrinsically linked with the national emblem of England.

(Bottom left)   'MME PLANTIER' An Alba rose whose blooms are sheer perfection in the 'old world' formation.

(Bottom right) R. gallica officinalis (Red Rose or French Rose) is another of the most ancient roses that has survived up until our present day.

(Top left)   'MAX GRAF' A true ground cover that will cover 3 to 4 metres across and flowers for several months.

(Centre left)   'QUATRE SAISON' (R. damascena bifera) was cultivated in Roman times, making it one of the earliest garden roses.

(Top right)   'MME. GREGOIRE STAECHELIN' (or 'Spanish Beauty') is indeed one of the most beautiful of the spring flowering climbers.

(Left)   R. fortuniana is capable of covering large sheds and climbing into trees, making a breathtaking display in early spring.

(Bottom left)   'MARECHAL NIEL' is a Noisette climber from 1864 which bears huge fragrant blooms throughout the year.

CHAPTER TWELVE

Fragrance

Hand a person a rose bloom to admire and, almost invariably, he or she will smell it to test the fragrance. I know that I do it myself. And if there is no fragrance, somehow I feel cheated. Such is the strong association between fragrance and the rose.

We speak of fragrance as though it were one single, simple factor. As you will soon see, fragrance is anything but simple. This, perhaps, is what makes it such an alluring part of the rose. Take the fragrance of the bloom itself, for instance. It is generally agreed that there are at least five basic scents — damask, orris, apple, lemon and cloves. Damask is the scent most usually associated with roses, a strong heady scent usually found in the dusky red tones of rose. Orris, (sometimes tending towards violet) is the rather sharp scent which seems to come through the copper-salmon roses. Apple would be familiar to all and it seems to have come through some of the climbing types. Lemon is a scent which occurs in so many other plants that it is not surprising to find it in the rose. Some of the paler tones of gold and pink seem to generate this rather elusive lemon scent. Clove is the sharp scent that some people would associate with the Tea roses.

Some people claim that they can separate many more scents such as violet, nasturtium, geranium, friesia, green apple, fruit salad, apricot and musk. Who are we to agree or disagree with this claim? For instance, some components of a fragrance are given off early in the life of the bloom while others are released as the blooms mature. Climate influences the fragrance too, for it is the soft warmth of the early sun which starts to evaporate the volatile oils that make the scent, but as the heat becomes more fierce (such as in Australia) the fragrance seems to dissipate as quickly as it is produced. This is why so many people claim that Australian roses do not have the scent that they could remember from plants in the northern hemisphere.

Fragrance

I have often heard it said that modern roses do not have the same strong perfume of old-world roses. Several studies indicate that this is not so. Many of the "old" roses, and here we are talking about roses of last century, did not possess much perfume. However, it is highly likely that this same lack of perfume meant that these scentless roses became less popular for this very reason, leaving the scented ones to remain over the following years.

On the other hand, the majority of today's new releases are fragrant, even the miniatures and cluster roses. Granted there was a time, twenty or thirty years ago, when fragrance was not considered to be important. Early Miniatures and Floribundas were usually scentless, while some colours in the Large-Flowered roses were often without scent, particularly the new orange-scarlets like 'Super Star', and some of the bright yellow and orange introductions. Today, you can find highly fragrant roses in every colour group of every type of rose.

However, I still have a feeling that the scent of the old-world rose was rather more simple and basic, whereas the modern rose, not unnaturally considering its long and involved breeding, is more of a bland mixture of many components.

So much for the fragrance that comes from the blooms. Be aware, however, that the foliage of all roses has its own characteristic, although slight, scent, in particular the 'Sweet Briar' (*R. eglanteria*) and its hybrids, which have a strong sweet and distinctive scent that is given off quite spontaneously during the warmth of the day. The 'Incense Rose' (*R. primula*) gives off the heavy scent of incense when the young leaves are bruised. Less well known, but equally distinctive, is the scent from the mossy glands of the Moss roses. This most closely resembles the smell of verbena, although it is not so pungent. When lightly touched or bruised, the "moss" will release the scent even more strongly and leave your fingers carrying the aroma for quite some time.

The complex chain of chemical reactions which creates the fragrance in both the blooms and the foliage is now fairly well understood. Less is known about the individual person's perception of the scent. It is not uncommon to hear quite strongly differing opinions as to the fragrance or otherwise of a certain rose, and it would be a foolish person, indeed, who takes sides in such an issue. As we have seen, the fragrance can vary throughout the development of the bloom and in differing climates. Add to these the human factor. I am sure that different people have different perceptions of scent; they find some blooms strong and others weak while a companion making the same judgement at the same time may arrive at a completely different assessment.

Nevertheless, the rose scent is there for you to enjoy, to inhale slowly and deeply, to almost drink in. Stroll through the garden on a balmy evening and try to isolate the fragrance of each variety of rose as you pass. Walk along the street, again trying to isolate the rose scent from other plants. Pick a fragrant rose just to have it near you in the home or in the office and to share with other people around you. Surely fragrance is yet another of the pleasures of growing roses.

CHAPTER THIRTEEN

Cutting and keeping blooms

Choice of varieties, conditioning blooms, packing

It seems so futile and wasteful to see blooms that have been freshly picked and carefully arranged into a floral piece droop and fall within a day when they have the potential to last so much longer. Of course, it does not help that our average temperatures are much higher than those of the major rose-growing areas in the northern hemisphere. High temperatures dramatically shorten the life of all blooms. So what can we do to get the most from our cut blooms?

Basically there are two points to consider — the choice of variety and the conditioning of the bloom.

Of course, if you have already planted your garden, that eliminates the first point, but if you are still planning your garden, then here are some guidelines. The largest blooms are not necessarily the best keepers contrary to what some people might expect. Generally, the medium-sized cluster flowered roses are good keepers and some miniatures are quite exceptional. More important, however, is the colour of the variety. Reds, pinks and whites are usually the best keepers with the yellows and bronze varieties being the shorter lived, while the copper, coral and scarlet-toned varieties are somewhere in between. The blue-toned varieties are fair keepers. Unfortunately, it is only possible to make generalized observations about the durability of blooms as each variety has its own natural cut life. Occasionally, particular varieties are far more durable than others in their colour group, and special mention is made of these elsewhere (see page 56).

On the conditioning of the bloom we can be more specific, for all varieties, be they long or short keepers, can have their lives extended by the use of a few simple treatments.

When a rose stem is picked in the bud it continues to grow for some time, perhaps for several days before it starts to decline. By ''growing'', it means that the stem gains weight slightly for a while, stops, then as the weight decreases to the

111

original weight the bloom starts to deteriorate. This increase in weight is brought about by the intake of water so that if the stem cannot take up water it immediately starts to decline. One must remember that the moment the stem is cut, the tiny sap-carrying capillaries start to suck in air instead of water, and within a few minutes air pockets are forming within these vessels. Once the air pockets exist the intake of water almost stops.

This leads to the first treatment. When cutting, carry a bucket of water with you and drop the stems into it immediately, or, if this is not practical, re-cut the stems under water as soon as you are able. In order to increase the ''drinking'' surface it helps to make an oblique cut with a sharp knife, or even split the stem. The water intake is easier if the water is warmed to air temperature and, of course, it must be clean and fresh.

Blooms should be cut in the cool of the day, preferably early in the morning, and left to condition for several hours, submerged up to their necks in water until you are ready to arrange them. The blooms are now in a fairly stable condition as the water stresses have settled down, and you can go ahead and arrange the blooms as you wish.

In order to keep the blooms ''growing'' for the duration of their vase life, they need a little nutrient solution and a little disinfectant or biocide to suppress the development of algae and other water impurities. These are most easily provided through one of the well-known commercial flower conditioning preparations. One of the most damaging factors in the life of a bloom is the development of algae in the water, which quickly and effectively blocks the water passages of the stem. Any loss of clarity in the water is a sign that the water needs changing, and, of course, you always change the water and thoroughly wash the container between use.

In the light of our current knowledge about the factors that make rose blooms last longer, many of the ''old wives'' customs have proved to have scientific basis. Charcoal, copper coins, and aspirin all have biocide properties, while splitting and scraping the stems increases the drinking surfaces. The addition of sugar to the water provides a source of nutrients to the blooms.

When the arrangement has been completed there is still more that you can do. Avoid placing the arrangement too close to a heat source such as a fireplace, a room heater or an air conditioner. Avoid warm draughts in the summer. Occasional spraying with clean water through a fine atomizer spray will reduce the rate of transpiration in the stems and blooms and will significantly increase the keeping life. The dew-like droplets on the blooms will also add that extra lustre to the appearance of the arrangement.

Blooms may be held for several days by storing in a mildly cool refrigerator (approximately 5°C) still keeping the stem in a good depth of water. However, the life of the blooms is somewhat shortened once they have been taken out of refrigeration and the blooms tend to lose their freshness and lustre if stored too long in this way. Nevertheless, there are many occasions when it is worth resorting to refrigeration.

Should you need to pack blooms for transporting any distance, here is the procedure.

Firstly, condition the blooms as previously described. Next, arrange the buds into small bunches so that they are nestled slightly below and between each other, something like a compact sheath of flowers. Any blooms that are starting to open should be packed so that the petals are held closed as much as possible. Line your packing box with barely moist newspaper and lay the bunches in the box, supporting each bunch with a roll of newspaper just under the heads. Lay more moist newspaper between and on top of each bunch, supporting each bunch with another roll of paper. If the box has to travel by public transport it will receive rough treatment. Therefore, see that it is well filled so that the blooms are held firmly no matter which way the box is laid. Mark the container "With care. This way up": spray the blooms and foliage with an atomizer spray before closing the lid. Polystyrene foam boxes, such as picnic boxes or fruit cases, make ideal containers in which to pack the blooms.

Princesse de Monaco

CHAPTER FOURTEEN

Floral arrangements

Containers, aids and accessories,
proportion, balance and scale,
texture and colour

One of the great joys of growing roses is to be able to cut a bunch of blooms, take it inside, and arrange the blooms to brighten the home. A floral arrangement, especially roses, can do so much for each and every room in the house. Roses are also perfect for the office, the restaurant, the hospital, and wherever people can see and admire them. And the arrangement does not have to be of an expert standard. A solitary bloom, or a hastily cut handful thrust into the first receptacle that is to hand, can still gladden the heart and brighten the day.

Good floral arrangements are just as much an art form as any other of the creative arts and only some of us are fortunate enough to have the natural flair to reach such heights. For the rest of us, the observance of a few basic principles, the knowledge and use of a few practical aids, and a little imagination will improve your efforts in floral arrangement to the point where you will surprise yourself, and you will not be ashamed of your efforts.

Look around you and consider what floral arrangements can do for your home.

Are you thinking of entertaining? What about a small low-spreading dish of roses on the dinner table, a formal bowl in the front entry, a vase on the bookcase or sideboard, a couple of buds on the bedroom dressing-table, even a floating bloom in the bathroom.

Are you holding a child's party? Place clusters of bright colours into any of the children's old toys that can be adapted to hold water, set tiny blooms around the birthday cake, float blooms in bowls. Let the children do the arrangements for themselves.

Every room and every occasion should suggest to you some way of using roses. The bedroom, or the sick bed, can be enhanced with a little fragrant spray of more muted colours. Use colour to catch the atmosphere of the occasion. Use different containers to create different effects — tall or spreading, old or modern, formal or just cute. Style your arrangements to suit the setting — large and formal, stark and modern, small and simple.

What do you do when the gardener of the family proudly brings a prize bloom for you to display? Or when the youngest carefully picks off the heads (with almost no stem!) for "Mummy to 'range". Keep two or three bud vases to show off that special bloom, and a shallow bowl in which you can float the stemless blooms.

These and other tricks are half the fun of arranging roses, but, like all things, we improve with practice, so that each arrangement should be used to extend your repertoire. Look critically at each piece in relation to the guidelines set down. Very soon you will find that flower arranging can be really good fun.

Containers, Aids and Accessories

"Containers" refers to the vessel which both holds the water for the arrangement and also provides the visual "base" for it. A container may be almost anything — a vase, a bowl, an urn, a specimen vase, or a receptacle of glass, pottery, wood, metal or plastic. You will gradually see that certain arrangements suggest the use of containers of certain sizes, textures and proportions, so it is useful to have a collection of various pieces on hand to suit each occasion.

"Aids" are the things that help hold the various pieces of the arrangement in the right place. The earliest aid was a crumpled piece of bird-wire fitted to the mouth of an urn or vase and, indeed, this is still used for deeper containers. For the past twenty years or more the pinpoint holder has been the main aid for use in the shallower containers, especially in the simpler, starker arrangements. The pinpoint is fitted into the container with a ring of plasticine pressed firmly into place. Both must be perfectly clean and dry when being attached. Blocks of a foam-like substance called "oasis" are a newer aid which hold their own water, and into which stems are easily inserted from any direction. Besides being useful for fitting into traditional urns and vases, these blocks may also be used as free-standing "containers", thus providing far more scope for impossible "containerless" arrangements.

"Accessories" are articles or materials which compliment the arrangement by making it look more complete or logical, or perhaps by suggesting the meaning of the arrangement. These may be anything from a mat beneath the container or a cloth draped behind it; pebbles or glass baubles in the exposed areas of the bowl; or small articles such as jewellery, toys or books which help to explain the theme of the piece.

Proportion, Balance and Scale

The basic proportion of container to arrangement is regarded as 1:1½. This means that the floral piece should be one-and-a-half times the height of the container, or, for a flat arrangement, one-and-a-half times the width. I say floral pieces because this is taken to mean the buds and tips of foliage and not just the main blooms. In fact, if you are not satisfied with the effect, try adding or subtracting such light

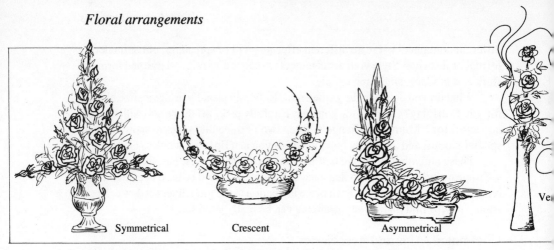

Symmetrical   Crescent   Asymmetrical   Ve

pieces of foliage and you will be amazed at the difference that it will make. As you develop more skill, you may successfully vary this rule somewhat, but for the moment it is a good starting point.

"Balance" refers to the visually satisfying effect that the arrangement has when at rest. If it **appears** that it wants to fall forward, backwards or sideways, even if you know that it is quite stable, it nevertheless worries the eye of the beholder and creates an impression of unrest.

There are a few tricks to achieving visual balance. Larger blooms should be placed lower down and to the centre, with smaller blooms and buds softening the outline. Even the tiny green buds help to lighten the extremities. Darker colours are visually heavy, and thus should be placed lower down or used to correct an imbalance. Flowers or foliage cascading down below and around the container give a more stabilizing effect.

Balance does not mean that the arrangement must be symmetrical. Assymetrical arrangements are just as effective provided that you group your visual weights either side of the apparent balance point of the container. For instance, a Lazy "S" or "Hogarth Curve" (see diagram page 117) arrangement will soon tell you if it is not in balance, but more dramatic asymmetrical arrangements may have a bold block on one side balanced against long light pieces on the other side.

"Scale" means that the piece is of an appropriate size for the setting or the occasion. For instance, church flowers or hall decorations need to be quite large, to be in "scale" with the setting. On the other hand, a table setting for an intimate dinner party needs to be low and small. A piece for the entrance hall often needs to be tall and flat against the wall, while a family room or playroom arrangement could be informal and low. A solitary bloom on a dressing-table is always just the right size.

Texture and Colour
These two factors determine whether the arrangement looks at ease in its surroundings.

Modern roses look right in most settings and with many different containers.

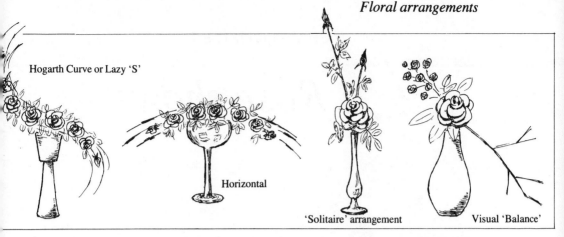

Hogarth Curve or Lazy 'S'

Horizontal

'Solitaire' arrangement

Visual 'Balance'

However, for lovely effects in older homes and cottages there is nothing like the old-world roses arranged in urns, crystal vases or silver bowls to emphasize their interesting shapes and muted colours. The single and species rose, on the other hand, suggest sparse, angular arrangements set in rough pottery or wood, and set against the brickwork or timber of the home.

Colours can set the mood of the room, with pastel colours in the bedroom or lounge; more strident colours in the kitchen, family room or sun room. The shape or line of the arrangement may be picked out with bright colours, the pastel tones making up the background and providing the contrast. A particularly lovely specimen bloom may be highlighted by the use of a background of softer tones.

Try not to mix all colours indiscriminately. For best effects, use one or other of the following:

- Use all tones or shades of the one colour, with possibly some neutral colour, such as green, to fill in or make up the background. This is known as "monochromatic" arranging.
- Use colours that are close to each other on the "colour wheel", for example, violet, mauve, red; or orange, yellow-orange, yellow. These are analogous. Again a neutral background is acceptable.

There is now no reason why you cannot create some surprisingly good arrangements. Use every opportunity to play with your roses — experiment with different styles and lines, pull the arrangement to pieces and try again if you are not happy, go back to the basic rules if the display does not seem to look right. Don't forget to use an accessory or drape, or perhaps raise the piece on a block to give it more character. Experiment, too, with the placement of the arrangement in the room. Can you feature it with a ceiling spotlight, or place it near a painting so that one complements the other? Perhaps the arrangement will add interest to a bare shelf or draw your eye towards a piece of fine furniture.

One parting word. It does not have to be the lady of the house who does the floral work. I know of several men who do not only enjoy working with roses and flowers but also excel at the art of floral arrangement.

CHAPTER FIFTEEN

Rose shows

We humans are competitive creatures. We are always trying to prove that we can do something better than the next person, be it flying to the moon or growing the biggest pumpkin! And so, too, it is with roses.

When we grow a magnificent bloom we must show it to everyone. But because the next person has grown an even better bloom, we must line them up in order to have them judged accordingly. There is your rose show.

Many rose enthusiasts find great satisfaction in striving for that perfect bloom. In fact, they make up a large proportion of the membership of rose societies. If you have ever attended a rose show, you have no doubt wondered why one bloom was selected above all the others. Judging criteria throughout the world are relatively consistent although there are some minor differences. For instance, in the U.S.A., blooms are "staged" or displayed as closer buds with a lot of emphasis given to the foliage and length of stem, whereas in the U.K. blooms are larger, more open, and usually without much stem exposed.

Judging standards in Australia and New Zealand are fairly consistent, especially since the start of regular international rose conventions, and the amalgamation of Australian state societies into an Australian society.

When visiting a rose show, what do you look for?

The prestige section is for "Exhibition" type blooms — the largest, most formal of all blooms. Next in order of prestige are the "Garden" types, which are generally similar to the exhibition blooms except that they should look as if they have been freshly picked from the garden, with side buds and foliage still attached and without obvious signs of having been dressed or "doctored". Most shows include a section for "Decorative" roses, which although easy to define, in practice are hard to put into their category. Decoratives are meant to be the simpler, semi-double roses, the beauty of which lies in their crisp simplicity.

118

There is a section for "Cluster Flowers", where the exhibit consists of a natural cut from the garden featuring a representative number of florets and buds, including provision to trim out spent blooms that would otherwise spoil the effect. As more and more Cluster Flower roses are becoming crossed with the larger roses, it is becoming quite a problem to place particular varieties into their correct categories. Some shows now call for solitary blooms as one class, and multiple heads as another class.

"Miniature" roses are a significant part of shows and are usually staged in a special area with sloping tiers and tiny containers in order to present their small size to best advantage. Solitary blooms and multiple heads are usually called for.

The section calling for "Full Blooms" (sometimes termed "Full Blown") always creates a display of colour. Blooms must be at their fullest point of opening before they start to decline. Many shows now include a section calling for blooms in three or four stages of development, from a bud to a full bloom, a true test for a rose that can be good from start to finish. There are, in fact, two factors in conflict here. The long, elegant buds are that way because they do not have many petals inside and thus they open rather loosely. On the other hand, the lovely, thick, full blooms with ample petalage, like 'Peace', come from thick, globular, rather blunt, buds.

Single (five-petalled) blooms, sprays of species roses, and cuts of "Old-fashioned" roses usually make up the balance of the rose cuts at a show.

Within the sections just mentioned, you will find particular groups or classes, such as "one bloom", "three blooms", "six blooms" and "twelve blooms", and even more. Here, some of the skill of exhibiting revolves round the grading and placement of the blooms within the set. Colours and sizes are carefully arranged in order to, perhaps subconsciously, win the favour of the judge. There, in summary, are the classes or groups of roses competing at the rose show. But, what was the judge actually looking for when she/he arrived at her/his choice?

One criterion states "the rose shall be at its maximum stage of possible beauty". This, of course, can be very subjective and dependent upon the personal preferences of some judges. It also means that some varieties might be considered to be more beautiful in an earlier or later stage of opening than other varieties. However, it is generally expected that the outer petals of the bloom should be fully extended while the inner petals are still folded into the characteristic spiral formation leading into a pointed centre.

The bloom should also have a circular outline, in other words, it should have opened evenly all round. Some importance is also attached to the way in which the petals open — evenly from inside to out without leaving gaps or "holes" within the arrangement of petals. And, of course, the bloom should be free of bruising and damage and should still retain its freshness and lustre, which is something that goes against a bloom that has been held in refrigeration for too long.

Such is the zeal to produce that perfect bloom for the prestigious "Exhibition" class that top exhibitors almost reconstruct their blooms by setting the petals into place with small pellets of sponge plastic which are removed just before the arrival of the judge. This technique produces magnificently formed blooms for the judge, but unfortunately, the blooms do not always keep this shape for long and visitors to the show are left wondering, at the end of the day, what has happened to the form of the champion bloom chosen earlier in the day!

For those of you who would like to try your hand at exhibiting, you should join your State rose society, where many of the members will be skilled exhibitors and will be only too pleased to help you get started.

Obtain a show schedule and study it carefully for this is virtually the "rule book" for the show. Make sure that you have the right type of rose in the right class. For most classes, fresh, clean, undamaged cuts will stand you in good stead. Obviously, signs of mildew, black spot, aphids and thrips will penalize the exhibit, so also will damage from chewing insects, tears by thorns and wind bruising. Some exhibitors will pull off one or two damaged outer petals or carefully trim a ragged edge, but a skilled judge can pick the unnatural effect of such treatment. If you choose to "pellet" your blooms into shape, be sure that you remove every one of the pellets before staging, as judges are very severe on such an omission.

The spent blooms on large clusters may be neatly removed, but it goes against you if such removal leaves an unnatural gap in the head of the blooms. Cut stems of generous length so that you can shorten them later if necessary. When arranging your cuts into the exhibiting tubes or bottles try to have all blooms looking squarely at the judge as she/he moves along the rows of exhibits. This means that the blooms in the back row should be tallest with a slightly inclined neck, while the blooms in the front should be shorter, with straighter stems, so that all blooms focus on the judge. Paper wads or scraps of stem will help you to hold the stems in the best position in the tubes.

Keep a record of the names of the varieties that you use, as most shows insist that you name each exhibit.

CHAPTER SIXTEEN

More than 'just a pretty flower'

Some recipes using rose petals and rose-hips

By now you could easily be excused for thinking that roses are just for decoration; to be admired as flowering plants in the garden or to be arranged as cut flowers. This is certainly not the case. Over the years, and especially in the Middle Ages, roses were used more for their herbal, medicinal and nutritional value than for their decorative appeal. Nor, as we may have expected, was this functional use confined to English-speaking areas. The whole area from Europe, the eastern Mediterranean and the countries of the Middle East, right through to India, were rich with ancient recipes for the many and varied delicacies to be made from roses.

Rose petals found their way into hosts of foods and potions, while the fruit (hips) of the more succulent species were also used. The most common base was undoubtedly rose-water, made by infusing petals in water. This was used for purposes as diverse as a refreshing drink, for garnishing a meal, or, in many instances, for sprinkling throughout the house to offset the unsanitary smells that were a part of life in those days.

Petals were also included in conserves, honey, jellies, tea and wine, while, in dried form, they formed the basis of pot-pourri. The valuable and exotic rose attar, the pure aromatic rose oil not to be confused with rose-water, is yet another extract from rose petals (an ancient process which persists to the present day). Rosary beads can be formed from petals, while decorative, incense-producing candles are yet another use of the petals.

Rose-hips, too, have been used in the production of syrups and purees. For centuries they have been valued as a source of nutrition, and this has been confirmed more recently when several essential vitamins have been extracted from the fruit. Hips are especially rich in Vitamin C, exceeding the concentration of the traditional citrus fruits by some fifty times. During World War II, volunteers used to harvest the wayside *R. canina* hips in Britain for processing to supplement their frugal rations. The same hips are readily available growing wild in Australia. However, the well-known *R. rugosa* is not only more ornamental but is three times richer in Vitamin C than *R. canina*.

Recipes Using Rose Petals

Rose-water

Nowadays, rose-water is often used as a flavouring in sweets and desserts, substituting for vanilla or almond flavouring. As the rose-water tends to lose its flavour through heating it should be added almost at the end of cooking. A half to one tablespoonful in an average recipe should be sufficient to add a distinctive flavour.

Rose-water can be made quite simply at home. Collect the petals from fragrant roses and place them in a suitable saucepan with a lid. Half to three-quarters cover the petals with water, then heat slowly until barely boiling. Remove from the heat and allow to cool, then strain into a clean receptacle.

Rose Petal Jam

Gather roses for jam as early in the day as possible, but after any dew has dried. Pull the petals from each bloom and cut off the white base as this part has a bitter taste. Wash to remove any spray residue and allow to dry on a paper towel.

Dark-red roses provide a strong flavour while the pale pinks are more delicate. Dark pink produces the closest to a typical rose flavour.

Jams must be cooked in enamel, stainless steel or glass pans and stirred with a wooden spoon to avoid the product from becoming discoloured.

To each cup of petals add 1 cup of water and 1 cup of sugar. Boil until the sugar hardens on the spoon. Add a few drops of lemon juice and a pinch of tartaric acid at jellying time to prevent the jam becoming bitter. Place the jam in small glasses or jars (already sterilized) and let it cool before sealing the containers with paraffin.

Rose Jelly

To 1 cup of rose petals (prepared as for jam) packed down tightly, add 1 cup of water and 2 teaspoons of lemon juice. Boil until the petals are a washed-out colour, then measure 1 volume of liquid to ¾ volume of sugar. Boil till scum rises to the top. Remove this scum and put the jelly into sterilized glasses or jars.

Rose Petal Honey

Mash 250 grams (4 firmly packed cups) of sweet-scented rose petals with a wooden masher. Boil in ½ litre of water for 15 minutes. Strain and add 1 kg of strained honey and boil down to a thick syrup. Pour into sterilized glasses and seal.

Rose Conserve

Prepare fragrant rose petals as for jam. To each cup of finely chopped petals add 1 ¾ cups of castor sugar. Put in a jar and cover tightly to keep out the air. Let stand for one month. By that time clear liquid will have formed on top. Pour this off to be

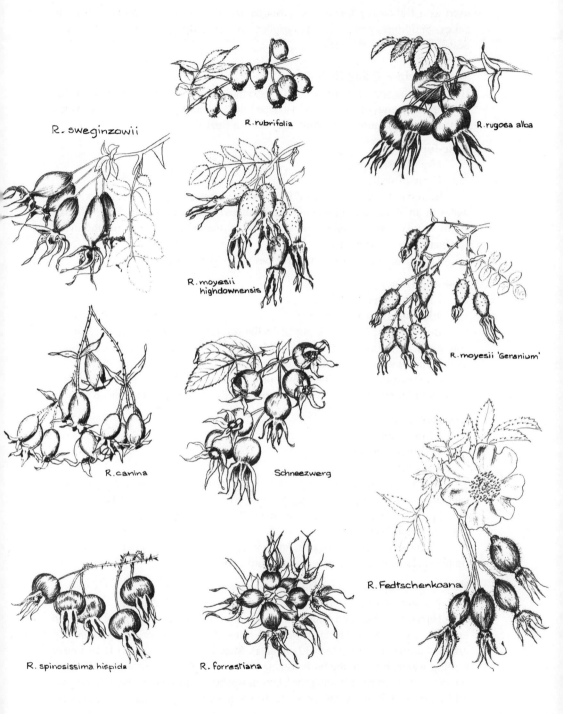

R. sweginzowii

R. rubrifolia

R. rugosa alba

R. moyesii highdownensis

R. moyesii 'Geranium'

R. canina

Schneezwerg

R. Fedtschenkoana

R. spinosissima hispida

R. forrestiana

123

used as a flavouring for sauces, custards and sweets. The solid part is used in cakes, puddings, pies, etc. 2 tablespoons of this pulp gives tang and aroma to desserts and whipped cream.

Some Recipes Using Rose-hips

Hips from the species roses are best, especially *R. rugosa* types, *R. macrantha*, *R. virginiana* and, of course, the wayside briar (*R. canina*). Harvest the hips when they are fully coloured but before they start to shrivel.

Rose-hip Puree

 1 kg of rose-hips
 1 litre of water
 Remove the calyx (withered flower ends) from the hips, place them with the water in an aluminium or enamel saucepan and stew until tender. This will take about twenty minutes and the lid should be on the saucepan. Then rub through a sieve and use as required.
 The puree is a basis for other recipes and may be preserved.

Rose-hip Honey

 1 litre of puree
 400 grams sugar
 Boil together until a skin forms on the surface of a test sample poured onto a cold plate. Pour into hot sterilized jars and seal immediately. Store in a cool dark place. The flavour is not unlike that of peach or tomato jam.
 One teaspoon of this honey will provide the daily requirement of Vitamin C for a child (approximately 40 mg) and two-thirds of the requirement of an adult.

Rose-hip Jam

 1 litre of puree
 ½ litre apple juice
 1 kg sugar
 Wash 1 kg of apples, cut into quarters, place in an enamel or aluminium saucepan with water just covering the fruit. Bring to the boil then boil gently until the apples are tender (about 20 minutes). Pour into a jelly bag or fine cloth and leave to strain overnight.
 Next day cook the hip puree, apple juice and sugar together until a skin forms on the surface of a test sample poured onto a cold plate.

Rose-hip Syrup suitable for Infants and Young Children

 It is important to remove the fine seed hairs by careful straining.
 Harvest the hips and remove the withered flower ends. Put 2 kg of hips in an enamel or aluminium saucepan with 1.5 litres of boiling water. Bring to the boil and boil until soft (about 20 to 30 minutes). Mash till pulpy then add 1 litre more of boiling water, bring to the boil, stirring all the time. Cook, then squeeze by hand through a fine cloth. Keeping the cloth unwashed, return the residue to the pan, add 1 litre of boiling water, boil 5 to 10 minutes, and again squeeze through the

'CANARY BIRD' is a hybrid species whose 60 mm blooms are produced over an extended spring season.

'SPARRIESHOOP' The large single blooms are firm and crisp, while the habit of growth is stout, hardy and attractive.

R. chinensis viridiflora (CHINESE GREEN ROSE) is actually a botanic deformity, but nevertheless is both attractive and useful. It flowers throughout the whole year and is often used in floral arrangements.

R. rugosa 'SCABROSA' The favourite variety of the most popular species roses, its blooms and heps are both highly ornamental.

R. chinensis mutabilis. The manner in which the blooms change colour as they open makes an interesting and airy effect.

R. spinosissima 'SINGLE CHERRY'. The spectactular blooms are followed by a heavy crop of shiny black heps.

(Left)   R. moyesii 'GERANIUM'. One of the brightest colours to occur amongst the species roses, its display of heps is equally eye-catching.

(Above)   R. stellata mirifica is one of the most curious of all, distinctly resembling the gooseberry in foliage and fruit.

cloth. Repeat the process a third time. Collect the three lots of squeezed liquid, put into a fresh, clean straining cloth, and allow the liquid to drip through. **Do not** squeeze. There should be more than 2 litres of liquid.

Boil the liquid, add ½ kg of sugar for every 1 litre and boil for 5 minutes while stirring. Pour the syrup into hot, sterilized bottles, seal with sterilized corks and, when cold, place hot melted paraffin wax round the cork.

Give 4 teaspoonfuls daily.

Pot-pourri

Pot-pourri is an excellent concoction made primarily of rose petals with added spices. Many wonderful benefits were claimed of it in earlier times but, nowadays, it is used mainly to add a characteristic "old world" fragrance to the room, or in the wardrobe, or as a simple gift.

In *Book of Physic*, by William Penn, pot-pourri was described thus: "To comport ye brains and for ye palsie, and for ye giddiness of the head. Take a handful of rose flowers, cloves, mace, nutmeg, all in a powder, quilt in a little bag and sprinkle with rose water, mixed with malmsey wine, and lay it in ye nod of ye neck."

Here is a practical modern-day recipe.

100 grams (5 cups) of dried rose petals

1 teaspoon of powdered orris root

1 teaspoon of cinnamon

1 teaspoon of nutmeg

1 teaspoon of allspice

Mix together and stir well. Place in a tightly covered jar, large enough to allow occasional shaking or turning of the petals during the six weeks' ripening period.

A few drips of oil of roses or rose perfume will strengthen the fragrance.

This is a basic mixture to which any other dried fragrant flowers, leaves or peel may be added, such as mignonette, jasmin, rosemary, lavender, geranium leaves, bay leaves, violets, carnations, mints and herbs, dried orange or lemon peel, crushed cloves and lemon verbena leaves.

CHAPTER SEVENTEEN

Photographing roses

General, close-up, exposure, lighting,
focusing, composition, prints
or transparencies

These days, so many people have high-performance cameras which are capable of taking good rose photographs that it is worth spending a few moments to help you to get the best results with your photographs.

General Views

Most cameras will make a good job of general views of rose gardens or even of individual bushes. It is essential to use colour film, as black-and-white photographs are a job for the expert if the results are going to look anything better than a shower of confetti. Try to include some feature besides the roses in order to give an idea of scale or size — paving, brick wall, turf, people or pets add interest and perspective.

Be critical of the background. It is so easy not to notice a power pole, a rusty fence, or weeds as you are focusing. Above all, see that you are not taking a view of your own shadow.

Contrary to popular belief, shots taken towards the sun are not only permissible but are usually more dramatic. The main requirement is that you read the exposure off the actual bush or flower that you are photographing without the meter taking in the brighter sky or sun in the background.

Decide primarily what you are taking and concentrate only on that, so that other objects in the photograph all help to draw attention to it, not detract from it. It helps to look at the view through almost closed eyes. This removes the fine detail so that you can see the basic composition all the more distinctly and thus judge whether the balance of the photograph will be correct.

Close-ups

I took my first rose close-up with a Kodak Retina with a supplementary lens. I used a piece of string tied to the front of the camera to get the focus correct. Later, I made a wire frame which fitted onto the camera and framed the field of vision for me. With such equipment photography was slow, uninteresting and inaccurate. Modern cameras have changed all that.

A single lens reflex (SLR) with either a close-up lens or extension tube is by far the easiest and best type of camera to use.

Exposure

Exposure is important in order to achieve accurate colours. For very dark (red) or very light blooms, take your light reading quite close to the bloom so that you are reading the exposure for the bloom only and not for the surroundings. For an automatic exposure camera this means that you must override the ''auto'' setting.

Lighting

Slightly overcast light gives shadowless effects with still plenty of brilliance in the bloom. The strong shadows of sunlight may be softened by using an in-fill flashlight, but I prefer to use a silver foil reflector to give just the right amount of in-fill lighting to soften the shadows. Shading the area with a piece of thin terylene curtain is another way of softening the harsh sunlight. Backlighting (that is, with the sun shining towards the camera) can be very effective. This applies especially when you are aiming at high blooms with the blue sky as background. However, this is a situation where it is vitally important to read the exposure of the bloom only, masking out the effect of the bright sky behind.

Focusing

The matter of focusing is more critical when working at close range. Try to arrange the blooms in a more or less flat plane to the camera, then use a fairly shallow depth of field (an open aperture) so as to blur out the background. Focus on the stamens or other fine detail, as flat petal areas do not look so obvious if out of focus.

Composition

My overall advice is ''be natural''. Solitary blooms are easy to take, but they tend to look uninteresting. It is much better to include a bud or two, or even two or three blooms in various stages of development. Photograph them as they are on the bush, if they are facing the right way and on a fairly flat plane. Otherwise carefully pull the branches together, or cut a bloom and tie it into place beside the others with a green twist tie or florist's tape. Be particularly careful to make the blooms and foliage lie naturally. Leaves usually face up and outwards, so watch that they have not become unnaturally twisted during your preparations. Fully open blooms look best almost full on, while buds and part-open blooms seem best viewed side on.

A fine spray of water gives a dew-like sparkle to the blooms, but don't do it to every photograph. It can become a monotonous technique. In the same way, an occasional bee which happens to settle on the bloom that you are about to photograph will add interest, but again, don't overdo it.

A technique which is used in portrait photography can be effective with large solitary blooms. By breathing softly on the camera lens to "fog" it, immediately before taking the shot, the result will be a delightfully softened effect — not out of focus but evenly subdued. You can get the same effect around the edges of the photograph by lightly smearing the perimeter of the UV filter (every camera should have one fitted, even if only to protect the main lens) with vaseline, leaving the main subject area clear.

Prints or Transparencies

Both forms give good results these days, so the choice is personal. How do you display your photographs? By showing them to your friends, by giving illustrated talks, or by having them used in magazines or books, you should probably use transparencies. If you prefer to keep photograph albums, or to pass your photographs around amongst a few friends, then prints are for you. On the other hand, transparencies are cheaper per photograph, and can be made into prints at a later stage if desired.

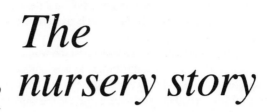

CHAPTER EIGHTEEN

The nursery story

Why propagate, under stocks, budding,

chip-budding, annual programme,

collecting budwood, purchasing nursery

plants, quality

As one who works closely with the production of roses I can easily take for granted the process of producing rose plants, whereas the layman may treat the subject with a certain awe and mystique. I can assure you that the process is relatively simple and I will tell you how it is done commercially in nurseries, although the same principles apply for the amateur grower.

You will appreciate that seeds, the result of cross pollinating two different roses, produce a seedling that is different from both parents. This is called bi-sexual reproduction. The other alternative is to take a piece of a particular rose and establish it as an independent plant, that is, to give it its own system of roots and branches. This is a-sexual (without sexual) reproduction, and the new plant is an exact replica of the mother plant. In its simplest form it is a rooted cutting, but it can also be achieved by layering, by division and, of course, by budding or grafting. However, there is an important difference. Cuttings, divisions and layering are all methods of establishing a piece of stem to grow on its own root system. Many roses grow very well in this way but just as many either refuse to grow or make only poor plants.

This leads us to the budding or grafting method. In this case, a particular rose, which is called the rootstock or the understock, is first grown to a suitable size, and then a portion of the desired rose is budded onto it, so that after some appropriate trimming and shaping, you have a plant which has the roots of one variety and the top growth of the other. I will endeavour to explain the most usual procedure, then tell you about some variations.

A typical rose nursery maintains what is called its "stool" bed, which is the source of its rootstocks. It looks like a tangle of wild climbing canes but it is certainly more than that. These rootstocks are especially chosen roses which must possess many criteria: they must take root easily, they must be able to form

131

vigorous healthy plants resistant to most diseases, they must be compatible with the buds that are put on them, they must form a fibrous root system for safe transplanting, they must live to a good age, and they must be able to withstand the various pressures of their locality such as summer heat, winter waterlogging, sandy soil or alkalinity.

Some time between April and August the whole rootstock is cut to the ground and the canes are selected and trimmed to give smooth straight cuttings, about the thickness of a pencil and between 250 mm to 350 mm in length. So that the cutting will not sucker, and also to provide a suitable area upon which to insert the bud, all of the "eyes" or axil buds, except the top quarter, are cut out with a sharp knife. Next, the cuttings are calloused in sharp sand for a few weeks before being planted out into the nursery field. There they take root and grow until, by late spring, there is a substantial head of growth on the top of the cuttings.

At the same time the nursery is looking to its source of budwood. Usually the nursery maintains a permanent bed of stock plants, or "mother" plants of each of the varieties that it wishes to propagate. Cuttings of budwood are taken from these although they are sometimes taken from mature nursery plants as well. The budding eyes used are the piece of current season's growth that has just borne flowers, and should be the section of the stem, not too high or too low, that bears the largest five or seven leaflet leaves. This usually involves discarding the top and bottom two leaves.

The nurseryman is constantly preoccupied with the factors of maturity and disease up to this stage. For a successful bud union, it is important that both the rootstock and the budwood are at a certain stage of maturity. The buds are "ripe" when the flowers on the "mother" plants have just fallen. If it is too soon, the wood is jelly-like and the cambium layer between the wood and the bark is greasy. When it is too old, the bark will not separate from the wood, and the cambium layer is dry and stringy. The rootstock is ready when the bark can be lifted from the wood without appearing to be too greasy nor too stringy and dry. Although an amateur can do his budding on the day that conditions are right, the nurseryman must endeavour to keep his beds in a state of readiness throughout the two or three months of budding season, starting late spring.

All virus diseases and many bacterial diseases are permanently entrenched in the plant once it becomes infected, so that the only recourse is to discard or "rogue" the infected plants, both mother plants or rootstocks, and replace them with healthy ones. A good nurseryman is constantly on the lookout for suspicious signs of disease, marking the plants or destroying them as the case warrants.

Budding

By far the greatest number of roses are budded by the 'T' budding method, as are most fruit trees. The budder uses a special sharp budding knife, which has a high-quality blade at one end and a blunt blade of fibre or bone at the other. The rootstock is wiped clean, a T-shaped cut is made through the bark on a smooth part of the rootstock some 20 mm to 30 mm long vertically, with the horizontal bar of the T cutting round a quarter of the circumference of the bark. Turning the knife round, the blunt end is used to lift the bark in the top corners of the T so as to form a pocket of bark ready to receive the bud.

The bud is cut from the stick with a long cut beneath the bud or eye, starting about 10 mm below the eye, going down to a depth of about one quarter of the thickness of the stick, and finishing the cut at a point considerably longer than the prepared T cut. Removing the sliver of wood that remains under the bud is a matter of practice and requires a soft touch. Holding the bud gently between thumb and forefinger, most budders use the point of their budding knife to lightly press away the tip of bark at the bottom. This enables them to grasp the sliver of wood between the knife point and their thumb and, with a gentle lift, to remove the wood. If the wood will not come away without distorting and tearing the bud, the chances are that the budwood is too old or too dry.

Rotating their grip on the bud, they slide it snugly into the pocket created under the bark of the understock. The eye should be in about the middle of the T pocket. The surplus length of budwood which remains above the T cut is cut off exactly on the horizontal cut so that the pocket closes neatly over the bud.

Finally, the budder binds the T cut area with special tape or a rubber band, leaving the actual eye protruding between the ties. Although the whole process may sound involved, in practice, a skilled budder would have put on five buds while you were reading this description. Most would put on 1000 buds a day with the help of a tier, while efforts of more than 4000 in a day have been recorded.

Budding is carried out from the time the first spring buds have matured, about late October, until some time in March, by which time winter dormancy has started in the understock and the bark will no longer lift from the cambium layer.

Can the average home gardener do his or her own budding? The answer is "yes". A sharp budding knife is most essential, for a blunt knife will bruise the bark and will not achieve an accurate bud slice. Judging the maturity of both the budwood and the rootstock is important but, above all, you will get much better with practice. Practise on waste pieces of stem, cutting both the T pocket and slicing the bud. Be gentle, for the bud is easily bruised, but also be quick as the cambium layer is drying while it is exposed to the air. Tie each bud immediately with a 10 mm strip of plastic budding tape (or cut your own from plastic carry bags). Commence below the bud with two or three turns, with another two or four turns above the bud, just leaving the bud exposed.

Chip Budding

There is another method of budding that is little used in nursery production, yet it is probably the easiest for the novice to use, and there is a good chance of success. It is called chip budding or sometimes bud grafting. This method does not rely as much on maturity or the separation of the bark from the wood as does the traditional method. Thus it is useful for budding out of season, or when either the rootstock or the budwood is especially dry or old.

With a sharp knife (any knife in fact that is not too flexible) make a

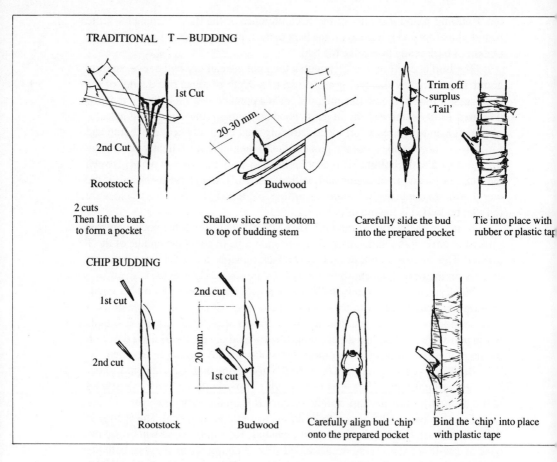

TRADITIONAL   T — BUDDING

1st Cut

2nd Cut

Rootstock

2 cuts
Then lift the bark
to form a pocket

20-30 mm.

Budwood

Shallow slice from bottom
to top of budding stem

Trim off
surplus
'Tail'

Carefully slide the bud
into the prepared pocket

Tie into place with
rubber or plastic tap

CHIP BUDDING

1st cut

2nd cut

2nd cut

Rootstock

20 mm.

1st cut

2nd cut

1st cut

Budwood

Carefully align bud 'chip'
onto the prepared pocket

Bind the 'chip' into place
with plastic tape

downward-sloping cut until you are about one-fifth of the way through the rootstock, then turn parallel to the bark and continue until the cut is about 20 mm to 25 mm long. Stop there, leaving the flap of wood hanging. Next, with a sloping cut, slice off the top half of the flap that you have made.

Turning now to the budwood, you make a chip which will fit as closely as possible into the cut that you have made in the rootstock. This is done by holding the budwood with the base of the stick towards you. The first cut is made towards you starting immediately below the eye and about a quarter of the diameter deep. The second cut starts about 10 mm to 15 mm above the eye, slicing parallel beneath the eye until it meets the first cut and the bud can be removed. Place the bud under the little flap of bark that you have created on the rootstock, being careful to locate the two surfaces as closely as possible on each other. Bind the bud into place in the same manner as with T budding, but be particularly careful that the bud does not move out of alignment when it is being bound into place.

In either case the bud tie is cut off sometime between two to four weeks after budding.

134

Annual Programme

The nurseryman would have one or two programmes in mind — yearling plants or second-year plants. Some warmer climates allow for the production of excellent plants in one year by planting the understocks before the depth of winter, (April and May); by budding during November and December; by cutting off the rootstock head above the bud at the same time as the budding tie is cut; and given suitable weather conditions, the plants are then ready to be dug for sale in June and July of the following year.

The second-year plants can start their programme later in the winter, often as late as September, for the budding does not have to start until January, through February and in some areas as late as April. However, the rootstock head is not cut off until the following late winter. In the meantime, the bud has lain dormant in the rootstock, thus the expression often referred to as dormant budding. These plants have the whole of the next year in which to develop, and ironically, one of the main problems of this programme is the prevention of the plants from becoming too large for easy handling and safe transplanting.

Once the rootstock head has been cut off, the bud growth is very rapid, and it is a constant chore in the nursery to pinch out the growing tip of every bud when it reaches 150 mm to 200 mm in length, so that the shoot is checked long enough to harden at the bud union and thus reduce the chance of blow outs.

If maturity is important at the budding stage it is also important at the digging stage, especially for yearling plants, and a nurseryman will adjust his fertilizing and watering programme in order to harden up the growth a couple of months before the plants are lifted for sale.

These procedures are just as applicable to you, the home gardener. More especially, you can afford to risk and experiment more as you often grow two or three times more than you actually need. However, you should beware of two things. Rootstocks that have suckered from a dead rose may very likely be diseased, as this disease, usually a virus, may have been the cause of the death of the original rose. In similar vein, a sickly rose which you may like to save may also be dying of a disease which will be transferred to any other rose that you may propagate.

Budwood

One day, you may wish to send some budding eyes to your favourite nurseryman to be grown especially to order. The procedure is quite simple provided that you observe a few important points.

Firstly, find out whether the nurseryman is agreeable to budding specials. They can be a disruption to his routine, your buds may introduce disease into his stock, or he may not have any suitable rootstocks at the time. So, check first.

As explained earlier, cut pieces of stem from beneath a flower that has just finished flowering. Remove all of the leaves, not by tearing them off but by cutting the leaf stem about 10 mm long, which then acts as a shield to protect the axil bud. Don't break off the prickles but snip off the points if they are troublesome.

135

Next, wrap the sticks of buds in **moist**, not too wet, newspaper, then in a film of plastic to prevent the paper drying. Of course, do not forget to label the contents. For sending long distances, postage or airmail is quite adequate, in which case you would roll the parcel into a tube of cardboard, or place it in a box strong enough to prevent the buds from being bent. The buds should carry safely for a week or more.

I have been referring here to sending buds anywhere within one country. Under no circumstances should you try to send budwood from one country to another, as such material must go through a rigid quarantine period, and there are other formalities to be seen to which vary from one country to another.

How to get your Nursery Plants

Let us now look at the question of how, where and when to get your supply of rose plants.

Let us assume that you intend purchasing your needs through orthodox channels, not by growing your own in one way or another. The two main sources of supply are from either specialist growers; or general nurseries, garden centres or chain stores. Practically all general garden suppliers handle rose plants in season. As they handle many other plant lines as well, it stands to reason that their range and their back-up advice is not as comprehensive as specialists, but they offer the advantage of "one-stop" shopping, conveniently close to your locality and they are usually cheaper in price. They usually rely on coloured labels to illustrate each variety, which is a help when making fairly straightforward selections. The quality of the plants is usually good especially when they have just arrived, but be cautious of plants that have been in stock for a long time, and any plants that have been kept in an airconditioned store.

Rose specialists, on the other hand, offer a wider range of varieties, especially in the area of new introductions; and special purpose roses such as stem roses, weepers, ground covers, border roses and "old-world" types. Most specialists grow their own plants so there is less chance of finding incorrectly labelled plants or plants that have deteriorated through excessive handling and poor storage. And, of course, you have access to the specialists' personal advice on rose queries and problems.

Although specialist growers may have their business some distance from the centres of population, they may provide mail order and delivery services to offset this disadvantage. They almost invariably have display beds of roses for public viewing, and will take orders ahead of time for supply to the customer at the appropriate time. Naturally, the cost of plants may be higher, which must be weighed against the benefits of the additional services provided. Although specialists are fewer in number, you can locate them through advertisements in such places as gardening magazines and telephone directories, and at gardening and rose shows.

Rose plants are available in two forms. Traditionally, they have been grown in nursery fields, dug in winter when they are dormant, and supplied as "bare root" plants. (This is something of a misnomer for a rose plant should not be left with ''bare roots'' for too long for fear of drying out!) The planting season extends from about May to August, by which time the plants have broken out of dormancy and therefore receive a set back when disturbed.

More recently, some growers have offered roses growing in containers, which can be bought and transplanted at any time of the year in the same way as other nursery stock. Miniatures are especially suited to being supplied in containers, although they are never meant to be grown for extended periods in the original container. In some cases you may find that the nursery has potted its unsold ''bare root'' plants. There is nothing at all wrong with this practice provided that the usual cultural techniques have been observed, but you may find that the selection is limited to what was left over after the winter.

Plant Quality

If you are buying rose plants for the first time you most probably feel like the proverbial ''babe in the woods'' when it comes to plant quality. You will be spending good money on what are unimpressive looking, dormant, prickly-looking sticks, and you are wondering just what constitutes good value or hopeless rubbish. Here are some points for you to consider.

Outward Appearances. The size of the plant is not an overriding factor, only a guide. It has been pruned back fairly severely to about 200 mm in the nursery, or it should have been, so don't be influenced by very long canes. However, the growth should be stout and nuggety. Multiple branches indicate that the plant is nicely mature but one good mature branch is still satisfactory. The root system should be fibrous. Occasional broken roots can be trimmed off as they will soon grow again. The main stem should be free of large scars and damage, although it is quite normal to see a number of small scars where the rootstock was 'de-eyed' in the nursery. The union of the bud to the rootstock should be healthy all round, without any areas of dead tissue.

Some people who are unfamiliar with the nursery budding process question the sharp angle or bend at this point. It is quite normal, and the plant will gradually develop all around and over the stem. Branches should not be shrivelled or pinched, although where only a portion of the plant has shrivelled it indicates that those particular branches are still immature, and provided that there are other harder branches as well, these can be cut out.

The branches of various roses take on different colours and effects, some even look quite dead. This is normal but, if you are in doubt, lightly scratch the bark with your fingernail and you should see green bark beneath.

Unseen Factors. There are a number of things that you cannot judge by just looking at the nursery plant, and it is then that you must rely on the integrity and experience of the nursery and the supplier. For instance, trueness to type — is the rose correctly labelled and budded from the best strain?; diseases, especially virus diseases, cannot always be seen in the young plant; and maturity, or hardening off ready for transplanting, will influence your plant-out success rate. (This can only be identified by an experienced grower.)

137

CHAPTER NINETEEN

Rose breeding

Professional breeding, plant variety rights, 'Do it yourself' breeding

Just as rose nurseries produce their roses by budding or, technically speaking, a-sexual reproduction (so as to maintain every plant as an identical replica of the original), so plant breeders aim to produce seedlings which are all different from their parents. The mature seed pods that develop on your roses in autumn, if planted, would each produce a range of entirely new roses, often remarkably different to the seed plant (and the pollen plant if this were known) from whence it came.

This, simply, is how a new variety of rose comes about; something that you or I can do just for the interest of seeing what will develop. But for the serious breeder it is not quite so simple.

For one thing, the breeder is not only trying to create a new rose bloom, he or she is trying to improve the whole performance of the rose. More continuous flowering, longer-lasting flowers, more resistance to disease, an improved habit of growth, more fragrance, and many other factors all combine to determine whether the new rose is distinctly better and worthwhile, or just another mediocre rose.

In addition, most modern roses are the end-result of generations of breeding, and have already reached a high level of perfection. So much so, that the major breeders of the world, of which there probably are twelve or more, calculate on sowing 50 000 to 100 000 seedlings each year in order to finally select, after four to six years of evaluation, barely six or eight good new roses. And the long road to the introduction into the rose catalogues of the world does not end there, for seedlings must be tested in other countries besides their homeland, then produced in sufficient quantities to meet the demand of the keen growers who wait each year to try the latest. In all, ten years may elapse from seedling to sale!

You may have made the mental calculation that the breeder's chances of success are about 1 in 10 000 (five successful seedlings out of 50 000). But there are other important skills required of the breeder other than the ability to produce masses of seedlings.

Before choosing the seed and pollen parents, considerable prior knowledge is required of their potential, and of the genes that are locked into their cells which are likely to emerge and contribute factors, some good, some bad, to the next generation. The breeder must know the mechanics of pollenating each flower by hand for a good chance of success, and must keep records of each cross for future reference. And of course, when the seedlings emerge, the breeder must decide which seedlings to keep and which to discard. This skill alone is very important for, obviously, the breeder cannot grow every one of the 50 000 to 100 000 seedlings to maturity so as to evaluate them. With experience and a certain intuition, he or she is able to discard perhaps 90 per cent within the first year. A tendency to disease, to lack-lustre colour, and too poor form or petalage can be identified in the early stage, and these seedlings must be discarded without a second thought. The remainder are budded onto understocks and planted into test beds in the nursery fields where they are grown under typical, if not harsher than average, conditions. More and more of these are discarded as faults become apparent, while the promising ones are increased in number ready for distribution to the breeder's agents around the world, and to a number of public trial gardens.

These trial gardens, and there is one or more in most of the rose-growing countries, are the fairest and most comprehensive means of assessing new roses before they are launched onto the market. A variety which scores well in a climate similar to your own is almost certain to be a worthwhile acquisition.

Plant Variety Rights. Considering the immense amount of skill, time and money that goes into developing new roses these days, it is small wonder that rose breeders have been among the first and largest users of what is known as ''Plant Variety Rights'' (a form of plant patenting) in those countries where that legislation is available to them.

At the time of writing, Australia is one of the last of the developed countries without such ''rights'', but the necessary legislation is currently before Federal Parliament, and when these ''rights'' become a reality, Australian rose growers can expect several improvements to the current situation.

Trial grounds will become a reality, for it is only when breeders can be guaranteed the security of their varieties that they will submit them to public trial. Without such security, any unscrupulous grower can ''pirate'' budding eyes and harvest something to which he or she is not entitled.

Rose breeding will become a proposition on the scale of overseas breeders, and this will be especially beneficial as the Australian climate is one of the kindest for this purpose. Not only will varieties be developed that are best suited to local conditions, but also Australia's name will become prominent as a creator and exporter of new varieties.

The cost of new varieties to the public, now extraordinarily high in the first and second year of introduction, will fall dramatically, for the breeder's royalty would be applied as a few cents on each plant over the ensuing fifteen years.

Overseas experience has shown the rose buying public that the slight extra cost of a "patented" rose is warranted because only the best roses, the ones that have the full confidence of the breeder, justify the extra cost of taking out a "patent". This is thus a reliable guide to the potential buyer.

"Do it yourself" Breeding. I have mentioned all of these points, not to scare you away from "dusting some pollen around" (as one breeder so quaintly puts it), but to give you some idea of the realities of rose breeding. My personal experience in this area is small, but I have had the chance to speak to many amateur and professional breeders, and to have studied the ideas and techniques of many others. Two points emerge.

If you take up breeding as a hobby, you will most certainly become "hooked". You will have a compelling urge to try and try again, year after year, completely preoccupied by the intriguing, if sometimes infuriating, pastime.

Secondly, don't expect results overnight. Many years will elapse before you start to produce reasonably predictable and presentable seedlings. Ten years will stretch into twenty years as the seasons fly past, and you anxiously await each year's batch of seedlings. If you plan to take up breeding as a retirement hobby, start your first crossings when you start your first job.

Methods of cross-pollinating vary from one breeder to another in detail only. The technique seems to be this:

- Plan your crosses beforehand, preferably having some plan or ideal in mind. If you understand the principles of genetics, so much the better, but it is not essential. If you can be sure that your seed parent is fertile, that is, it sets seed pods, then it will save you unnecessary and fruitless work.
- Do your pollinating in the spring so as to give the seed pods a chance to ripen by autumn.
- Wait until the blooms on the seed parent are about to unfurl. Pull off all of the petals, exposing the circular stigma in the centre surrounded by rows of fine yellow anthers. The anthers produce the pollen, while the stigma receives the pollen when it ripens to a sticky texture. At this stage, cut off all of the anthers with fine scissors or tweezers. This will prevent the bloom from being accidently fertilized by its own pollen. If you need the pollen later, drop the anthers into a clean dry jar or paper bag. Cover the emasculated bud with a paper bag to prevent accidental fertilizing by attentive insects.
- Within one or two days the stigma should become sticky and glistening in appearance. It is ready to receive the pollen.
- Meanwhile you should be collecting pollen from the desired pollen plant just as the bloom is opening. Cut the anthers into a clean dry receptacle and within a couple of days the ripe pollen will fall from the anthers and is ready for dusting onto the stigma of the seed parent. Generally this is done with a fine brush touched into the pollen deposit and then onto the stigma. The tip of the finger will also suffice. When you change to another variety of pollen, be sure to use a fresh brush or thoroughly clean it in methylated spirits. Re-cover the seed parent again with the paper bag for a few more days to prevent other accidental

pollinations, then it is safe to remove the bag.

Some breeders prefer to cut off the head of the pollen parent, remove the petals, and tie it upside down over and within the paper bag of the seed parent, so that the ripening pollen merely falls down onto the waiting stigma.

- Be sure to label each cross with the pollen parent, and also the seed parent (for this will eventually be taken from the bush) and the date.
- Within two or three weeks the calyx or seed pod will start to swell noticeably, indicating a successful cross.
- The seed pod is ripe for harvest in late autumn when it starts to turn from green to its autumn tones. Collect the pod and store it in a box or tray of moist peat, perlite or vermiculite. Store the box in a cool spot, and if you do not have deep frosts in winter, place the box in the refrigerator for a few weeks at a time to simulate winter chilling.
- By August, the seeds are ready to plant out into seed trays. Carefully remove the seeds from the pods, discarding undersized ones. Fill the seed trays with sterile potting soil, and place the seeds in a grid pattern about 30 mm by 30 mm apart, then cover with another 10 mm of potting soil. Covering the box with a sheet of glass or plastic will speed germination until the weather warms up.
- As the seedlings emerge and begin to show their first flowers, about November, the difficult task of culling the inferior types begins. Some are obviously of little use and should be cut out rather than pulled out lest they disturb the nearby seedlings. As culling proceeds, be prepared to take the tiny stems of the promising ones and bud them onto understocks in your little nursery that is ready and waiting (see 'The Nursery Story', p. 141). It is only after the seedling has been transferred to an understock and has been observed for several years that you can get any reliable idea of its potential worth.

As the seedlings enter their second and third season you will already be making plans for your next batch that will, you confidently believe, overcome all of the faults that you have found in that year's batch. And so the fascinating and never-ending quest goes on.

CHAPTER TWENTY

Naming roses

Reasons, rules, identifying roses.

Obviously every rose that goes onto the market must be known by a name. Often the choice of that name spells the difference between the success or failure of that rose, so it may be of interest to look at some of the less-obvious aspects of rose names.

By the time a new rose goes onto the market it will have had at least four names. The sequence goes something like this. As a seedling, maybe one of 10 000 for that year, the breeder gives each a series of numbers or letters which identify the two parents, the year of the crossing, and any other information that the breeder considers important. For instance, Meilland's famous 'Peace' was originally known as 3-35-40.

After about two or three years of trials, perhaps fifty of the most promising seedlings (the ''short list''), are selected for further trials. So as to identify them more easily, they are given ''nicknames'', which may be any word at all, usually selected alphabetically straight from a dictionary. This name stays with the seedling for perhaps another five or six years, by which time the breeder has selected the four, six or eight varieties that he or she is going to release for sale. At this point, the breeder selects an official varietal name which, by international agreement, consists of three letters identifying the breeder, followed by other letters which make up a fabricated name. Meillands, for instance, is identified by MEI, Kordes by KOR, Harkness by HAR, and so on. This is the officially registered name that identifies that rose throughout the world.

Finally, the rose is given its commercial name by which you and I will know it in our country. I say this because there is an increasing tendency for rose names to be chosen to suit the whims and fashions of certain countries, and the rose may very likely have another name in another country. Much as this is against the interests of good nomenclature, it is now a commercial fact of life which the rose world has accepted quite philosophically.

(Top)   'Old world' roses have an undeniable charm. Their muted colours blend with never a discordant note.

(Centre)   'ANGEL FACE' One of the most charming of the 'blue' roses, arranged to perfection.

(Bottom left)   Pride of Show. An exhibit of 12 blooms. No mean feat to prepare such uniform and perfect blooms.

(Bottom right)   'BABY DARLING' Miniature in all respects. The container and blooms must be in proportion.

The American Rose Society undertakes the task of registering all new rose names and, to this end, an average of 200 varieties is recorded each year. Each three to five years this Society publishes a reference book, called *Modern Roses*, now in its eighth edition, which not only records the varietal name, but also the classification, breeder, introducer, date of introduction, parentage when known, colour, and growth habit, and any significant awards bestowed on it. Roses remain listed until such time as they are known to be out of commercial production and of no significant value as a record. The latest *Modern Roses* edition lists more than 12 000 names.

When a rose name ceases to be on this official register it may then be released to be used again on another new variety. This is why you may sometimes come across names which you feel sure you have heard before.

The "International Code of Nomenclature for Garden Plants" makes the following recommendations with regard to plant names, which of course includes roses.

- Species names should be printed in italics showing the genus, species and varietal names in that order, e.g. *Rosa chinensis minima*.
- Common names should appear within single quotes, e.g. 'Iceberg'.
- Names should not exceed two words, or at the most, three (not like the record-breaking 'Donna Maria do Carmo de Fragosa Carmona!).
- Names should not exaggerate the quality, like 'Surpasse Tout'.
- They should not be too general.
- They should not be too similar, e.g. 'Helen' and 'Helene'.
- They should not begin with an abbreviation, e.g. 'Conrad Ferdinand Meyer', not 'C. F. Meyer'.

With literally tens of thousands of rose names listed, it is small wonder that breeders are having to resort to some rather unusual names!

On the other hand, a count through *Modern Roses* shows that some prefixes are rather overworked; 'Mme' has been used more than 400 times, 'Mrs' more than 300 times, 'Golden' more than 200 times, 'Red' 'Rouge' or 'Rote' almost 150 times, and 'White' more than 120 times.

Some breeders used to love using their own name, such as 'McGredy's Yellow', 'McGredy's Sunset', etc., seventeen of them in all, while the breeder Poulsen associated his name with more than twelve of his new roses.

Other breeders adopt a theme such as David Austin's characters from *The Canterbury Tales*, and Jack Harkness has drawn on the characters of King Arthur's Knights of the Round Table. Kings and Queens, presidents, artists, singers and sportsmen and women have all been recorded by a rose name. Even commercial

'BLOOMFIELD COURAGE' weeping rose. Although only a spring flowering variety the effect is breathtaking for several weeks.

Roses can grace the smallest and most simple home. Battery Point, Hobart.

'TAMANGO' A fine example of a specimen bush — symmetrical, compact in habit, well clothed with foliage, plenty of blooms.

Many old roses still thrive amongst cemeteries and deserted buildings. Rookwood Cemetery, Sydney.

interests lend their names to roses — 'John Church' (shirts), 'Chrysler Imperial' (cars) and 'Daily Sketch' (publication) are some examples.

Identifying Roses

You may at some time find a rose which you wish to identify. If it is a recent rose which is still in commercial use you will need to take the bloom along to one of the major rose shows or to a rose society meeting, or take it to your usual rose specialist. The average garden centre staff may be unable to help you unless the rose is particularly well known.

However, we run into problems if the rose is a fairly old variety, for we must remember that many varieties have been coming into the country every year since the turn of the century. A few have remained indelibly in people's minds, but most have passed and been forgotten, so that it is only when a grower has actually grown and become familiar with the variety that he or she can remember it years later.

Which brings us to the situation which I meet many times a year. It is almost impossible to identify a rose starting from scratch. You must have some lead to go on. I can usually put the rose into its classification and approximate period, but if I have to rely on descriptions and photographs for reference, unless the variety is especially distinctive, any name that I venture can only be a calculated guess. I am sure that these remarks would be endorsed by other rose specialists.

When preserving a rose for identification it helps if you remember these points:
- Be sure to include some leaves, stem and prickles besides two or three stages of bloom.
- Try to gain some idea of the bush's size and habit, and whether it is a climber or not.
- Remember to describe the type of district, and the bloom's location in the garden (whether in shade or sun).
- Do you have any clues as to its age, its origin, or its supplier?

When sending blooms for identification, for instance, through the post, it is far more satisfactory to press the specimens as you would for herbarium specimens than to try and maintain them in their fresh state. Pressing is quite simple. You merely lay the specimens out in an orderly manner between sheets of newspaper and enclose them between the pages of a heavy book for a day or so, to absorb surplus moisture.

CHAPTER TWENTY-ONE

And now to the future . . .

We have seen the rose develop from its humble beginnings to the plant of today. You may logically ask "What will the future bring?" Obviously, no one knows for certain.

We know what breeders are working on, we know what is in the pipeline, so to speak, and we hear of what the breeders hope to achieve. From this we can extrapolate the trends for some time to come, perhaps ten to twenty years, and come up with some forecasts.

Let us first look at the colours — the aspect that seems to interest people most. No, I cannot see a black rose being developed and I cannot imagine that it would be attractive either. Nor can I see a true delphinium blue rose for many years, if ever. Such a blue is not a naturally occurring colour in roses and so can only occur through a major mutation. In any case, such a blue would take some getting accustomed to. I believe that other colours will become more brilliant, especially in the yellow-orange-scarlet range, and if there is to be such a thing as a new colour, it will be in the tones of brown, biscuit, ginger and bronze. But, more importantly, I can see more mixed colours coming into being. Margined edges, striped and splashed petals, reversed or bicolours, and "suntanning" colours will become the trend. Tinges of green are by no means unlikely.

The form of the flower will become more varied. The "typical" rose will become longer in the bud and be more decorative when open. Under the influence of earlier floribunda breeding, more varieties will produce their blooms in clusters, while more unusual forms such as rosettes, cup-shapes, ruffles and wavy petals will be represented. Fragrance will become more general throughout all types and colours.

So far as the rose plants themselves are concerned, the typical sized bush rose will still form the basis of the garden. However, to accommodate the trend towards

147

smaller gardens, and the gardens of units and apartments, many smaller-growing varieties will appear. These will be tough and colourful, and will grow equally well in pots, in window-boxes, indoors or outdoors. Smaller-growing climbers will be developed to accompany these "patio roses". In addition, I can see a number of special purpose roses being developed for such uses as ground covers, minimum maintenance hedge plants, and border roses such as the popular 'China Doll' to rival the annual bedding plants.

Probably the greatest improvement that you and I will welcome will be that of growing performance. Tomorrow's roses will literally not stop flowering, the new buds will be forming as the old flowers are falling — a trend that is already evident in some recent varieties. Secondly, there will be a slow but steady improvement in the natural disease resistance of the plant. Already certain varieties have good resistance to either mildew, blackspot or rust, so the potential is there, difficult though it may be, to bring these resistant strains all together in the one rose. Control of insect pests will become easier and less hazardous with the development of predators and insect repellants. Already spider mites can be controlled by predators, while garlic extracts have been proved to suppress aphids populations. Rootstocks could well be developed which have resistance to nematodes (a problem in sandy soils). What would be good news indeed for rose growers would be a rootstock tolerant to saline water, a weakness which is one of the chinks in the rose's armour. I believe that not much has been done in this area and yet salt tolerance has been bred into other plant families.

The current interest in the old-world roses will probably level out to being a significant, if only a minor, part of the rose scene. In fact, many new roses will include the characteristic forms of the old coupled with the performance of the new.

If my crystal ballgazing is correct, the rose in the twenty-first century will still be the "Queen of Flowers", riding through the peaks and troughs of popularity experienced by other plants, and giving pleasure to an ever increasing number of people who will enjoy them for one or all of the many reasons that have been mentioned in this book.

Index